NTC SKILL BUILDERS

WHAT YOU NEED TO KNOW ABOUT

DEVELOPING STUDY SKILLS, TAKING NOTES & TESTS, USING DICTIONARIES & LIBRARIES

Marcia J. Coman
Kathy L. Heavers

National Textbook Company
a division of NTC Publishing Group • Lincolnwood, Illinois USA

Acknowledgments

Grateful acknowledgment is made to the following for permission to reprint copyrighted materials:

Houghton Mifflin Company, for dictionary excerpts. Copyright © 1983 by Houghton Mifflin Company. Reprinted by permission from *The American Heritage Dictionary*, paperback edition.

H.W. Wilson Company, for *Readers' Guide* excerpts. *Readers' Guide to Periodical Literature*, July 1988 issue, copyright © 1988 by The H.W. Wilson Company. Material reproduced by permission of the publisher.

Photos: Steve Gottlieb, pp. 17, 23, 50; Larry Risser, pp. 2, 12, 21, 34, 37, 46, 63, 64, 69, 72.

Illustrations: Sandra Burton

Text Design: Linda Snow Shum

1995 Printing

Published by National Textbook Company, a division of NTC Publishing Group.
© 1991 by NTC Publishing Group, 4255 West Touhy Avenue, Lincolnwood (Chicago), Illinois 60646-1975 U.S.A.

4 5 6 7 8 9 VP 9 8 7 6 5 4

Contents

Developing Study Skills

DEVELOP (di vĕl' əp), v. To evolve to a more complete state

STUDY (stud'e) n. The pursuit of knowledge

SKILLS (skĭl) n. Proficiency, expertness

Were you ever taught *how* to study? Instructors often assume that students beyond grade school know and use good study techniques. You may know some people who seem to be able to do more in less time, and get good grades besides. How do they do it?

In this unit you will learn some simple techniques that good students consider most important when studying. Now you can discover some of their secrets.

Activity 1–1
Previewing Your Textbook

Learn to *preview your textbook*, and you'll be on your way to becoming a better student. By spending no more than five minutes the first day of class to preview each of your new texts, you can determine what material will be covered in the book, how familiar you are with the material, and how difficult the material will be for you. In addition, you will discover the book's format and the aids included to make your job as a student easier.

You can practice the technique now. Using a separate sheet of paper and this textbook, answer the following questions. Your answers will become your five-minute preview of this text.

1. List the title of the text.

2. List the author(s).

3. What is the text's most recent copyright date?

Previewing your text-
book makes studying
easier.

4. Read the Table of Contents. How many chapters are in the text? How many pages are in the text? List the title of the chapter that sounds most interesting to you.

5. Thumb through the book. Are there pictures? Graphs? Maps? Charts? Illustrations? Questions at the end of the chapters? Pages with a lot of white space?

6. Evaluate the difficulty of the text; how hard to you think this text will be for you to read and understand?

7. Turn to the end of the text. What appendixes does it have?

Activity 1–2
What Is "Previewing"?

Now that you actually have previewed a textbook, read the following article, "How to Preview Your Textbook." Using a separate sheet of paper, start a section of notes and entitle this section "Study Skills—Previewing Your Textbook." First, list the seven steps in previewing your textbook. Then, in your own words, answer the questions:

1. How do you preview your text?

2. What is the value of previewing your text?

How to Preview Your Textbook

The difference between being a good student or being a poor one sometimes hinges on whether you know how to study. There are some very basic study techniques that require only a short amount of time to learn, but that result in tremendous benefits. Previewing your text is one of these techniques.

Previewing your text involves looking at a book before a class begins to determine what the text contains. This process will take no more than five minutes, but in that amount of time you will gain much useful information. Your preview can reveal what material will be covered in the book and in the class, how familiar you are with that material, and how difficult that material will be for you to read and understand. You will be able to determine the following: the format of the book; the location of the study aids, pictures, charts, and graphs used throughout; and your level of interest in the material. Equipped with this information, you are a more informed and prepared student already, and you will save yourself study time later on.

The first step in previewing your text is to look at the title, author, and date of publication, or copyright date. The copyright date is important because it not only tells you how current the information is, it also tells you how popular the book has been. A book that has been printed and reprinted several times is usually a very popular one.

Next, read the preface or introduction. It usually discusses the scope of the book and explains why the authors wrote it.

Third, find the table of contents and read the chapter titles, main headings, and subheadings included within. Turn these into questions so that you can read with a purpose to find the answers.

Then, flip through the book, looking at any charts, pictures, captions, and graphs. These items provide additional information about the subject and also affect your interest in reading the text.

Fifth, evaluate the difficulty of the material. How much do you already know about the subject? How much does it interest you? Is the print large or small? How much white space does a typical page have? Are there many pictures, charts, graphs, and illustrations? These factors all determine the level of difficulty of the text and the amount of material you will have to read.

Next, know your purpose for reading the text. Are you required to read it for class? Will the teacher test you on its contents? Or is it just a supplement to the teacher's notes? Knowing your purpose is crucial in determining how and at what rate you should read the text.

Last, go to the back of the book to see what study aids are included. Does the text include a glossary of words and their meanings to help you with vocabulary? Is there an index listing names, events, terms, and the pages on which the items can be found? Better yet, does the appendix have solutions to problems you have been asked to solve? Obviously, all these materials will help you as you read the text, *if you know they are there*. If you don't spend time previewing your text, however, you may not discover them.

Activity 1–3
Study Setting Worksheet

Take a look at where you study, how you study, and what your "study center" consists of. How strong is your power of concentration in this environment? It may surprise you to learn that your study center, your study environment, and your method of studying directly affect your concentration and comprehension.

For a few minutes, think about your own study situation and environment. Then, on a separate sheet of paper, list the conditions that make it hard for you to concentrate. Be honest—no one will deduct points if your study area is a disaster! Be sure to leave room to jot down later your solutions to any problem conditions.

STUDY SETTING WORKSHEET

Conditions That Make It Hard For Me to Concentrate	Ways I Can Improve Those Conditions

Activity 1–4
Tips on Concentration

Read the following article, "Tips on Concentration." Then, add to your notes on study skills at least seven tips for improving your study environment, study techniques, and concentration.

Tips on Concentration

Think about your usual study environment. Are you sprawled on your bed with the stereo blaring, books and papers scattered around you? Are you trying not to spill the Coke when you retrieve that elusive pencil? Or is it, perhaps, flat on the floor on your stomach, in front of the TV, with the dog licking your ear and your brothers playing "invaders from space" nearby? If this sounds at all familiar, you may find concentration—or the lack of it—one of your biggest hindrances to effective studying.

"But," you ask, "how can I concentrate better?" The following tips have been gathered from students who have learned to do so.

Study in the same place every day. Psychologically, this establishes a pattern that your brain will respond to automatically when you settle down in that spot day after day. When your study place is your bed, the desire to study is in conflict with the desire to sleep, which often causes problems for many students.

In spite of what you may think, studying in a quiet place is more beneficial than being surrounded by music or other noise. From experience, you know you can learn to block certain sounds from your consciousness, such as the exasperated tone of your mother's voice calling, or the rumble of passing traffic. But having a quiet area is critical, because comprehension rates zoom downward in direct relationship to the amount of sound in your environment. Some experts assert comprehension can actually be cut in half!

Since your primary occupation at this time is that of student, make your "office" a study center. Gather together all the equipment you need to do your work. Face a blank wall if possible; don't let distractions creep in to break your concentration. After all, this is where you do your work.

Good lighting and ventilation are primary requirements when you set up your study area. Invest in a desk lamp that will eliminate glare and uneven lighting. Open the window a crack, even in chilly weather, to fend off stuffiness and the yawns that quickly follow.

Have a working surface that is large enough for your needs, and clear it of any clutter. Be sure to provide room for the supplies you need— perhaps just a shoe box on the floor beside your working area.

Remember, too, that your eyes will see more easily and become less tired if you prop your book up at a 30-degree angle, rather than leaving it flat on the desk top. Either hold your book at an angle, use other texts as a support, or build a book rest.

You will concentrate better if you have only one task before you at a time; too many tasks may overwhelm you. Always complete one task before beginning another. Avoid the urge to get something to eat or to call a friend. Instead, use these well-known stalling techniques as rewards for yourself when you have completed a task. With a definite plan of attack, you'll finish with all your assignments sooner.

Learning to concentrate is hard work, but the payoff is better grades. Good students have mastered this skill. You can too!

Activity 1–5
Solutions to Study Setting Problems

Now, consult your list of conditions that make it hard for you to concentrate (Activity 1–3) and think of some practical solutions to your problems. List the solution opposite the corresponding problem.

For the next week, put your solutions into practice. See how successful you are, and be persistent. Remember, it takes time to change habits. Then evaluate what did and did not work for you. Decide what permanent changes you can make to improve your study setting.

Activity 1–6
Where Does Your Time Go?

It seems we never have enough time to accomplish what we want to. Are you good at disciplining yourself to use your time wisely? Each day, how do you spend the sixteen hours you are not in school?

Consider the fact that the average kindergarten graduate has already seen more than 5,000 hours of television by age five or six. That is more time than it takes to get a bachelor's degree from college! How much time have you spent in front of the television? Perhaps you don't realize where your time really does go.

On the other hand, you might know someone who *always* comes to class prepared, who studies sufficiently for *every* exam, who carefully prepares *each* written assignment, and who comprehensively reads the text material. Do you envy that person as you scramble before class to get your work done, however haphazardly? If only you had more control of your time . . . .

Tracking Your Time

To help you pinpoint what you really do with your time, on a separate sheet of paper make a chart like the following and complete it according to your schedule for *one typical day in your school week.*

Start with the time you generally awaken, and continue to identify how you spend your time throughout the day, right up until when you usually go to bed. Include hours spent dressing, eating, traveling to and from school, attending classes, visiting, exercising, working, studying, watching TV, talking on the phone, sleeping, and so on. Make sure your log represents a twenty-four-hour period.

Time	Activity	Time	Activity

Now answer on your own paper the following summary questions:

1. How much time do you use to eat and dress?

2. How much time do you spend traveling to and from school?

3. How many hours do you attend classes?

4. How much time is used for exercising?

5. How much time is spent watching TV, visiting, or just relaxing?

6. How many hours do you work at a part-time job?

7. How many hours do you sleep?

Activity 1–7
Controlling Your Time

What did you discover when you used the chart to determine how you spend your time? Many people feel that they waste time, but they don't know how to correct the problem. The following article, "Tips for Control of Your Time," is written to give you some time-budgeting suggestions. Read it, and add to your notes on Study Skills one key idea from each paragraph.

Tips for Control of Your Time

Controlling your time is somewhat like learning to budget your money. At first, the money always runs out before the month ends, but with practice and planning, your money management skills increase. Just so with budgeting your time!

If you want to be in control of your time, a plan is vital. Your survival depends on it. Think about the things you must accomplish and decide approximately how much time you need to do them. Write these down; they provide a guide or budget for spending your hours and minutes.

Are you most alert in the morning or at night? This is important to know, because you should plan your study time accordingly. You will accomplish far more if you study when your concentration abilities are sharp.

Think about your study sequence. Hardest assignments to easiest? Alternating activities such as reading, then drawing a map, then back to reading? You may prefer the first-things-first method, finishing the most important projects before any of the others, and risking the possibility of leaving some things undone. Each of the study sequences mentioned here is used by successful students. As personalities vary, so do study sequences.

You'll be pleased to know that you *should* allow yourself breaks as you study. Some research suggests taking breaks of approximately ten minutes every hour. The best time to do so, of course, is between tasks. Breaks rest your mind and your eyes.

If you like structure, set up your time budget in an exact time frame. If, on the other hand, you dislike rigid time limits, plan your sequence without specific time allotments. Either approach can be successful, but remember that a time budget, like a budget of dollars and cents, must be somewhat flexible. It is sometimes hard to judge how long a task will take. If you can't meet the time requirement that you have allowed, revise your schedule. Because unexpected things come up, try to have some time in reserve, if possible.

If your out-of-school life is always in a state of chaos, devote a few minutes daily to sequencing your tasks. By having some plan, whether it be closely structured or more loosely organized, you will know the satisfaction that comes with gaining more control of your time.

Activity 1–8
Budgeting Your Time

Can you see from Activities 1–6 and 1–7 any areas where you might be able to adjust your present schedule in order to use your time more efficiently? List them on a separate sheet of paper.

Then create another chart like the one in Activity 1–6 for a schedule in which you will plan ahead. For the next week you are to create a new budget for your time. Keep in mind the best ways to use your time; your goal is to be more efficient.

At the end of one week, evaluate your new schedule. Did you succeed in using your time more to your advantage? If you found you were more prepared and less rushed, you will probably be eager to make your trial schedule changes permanent.

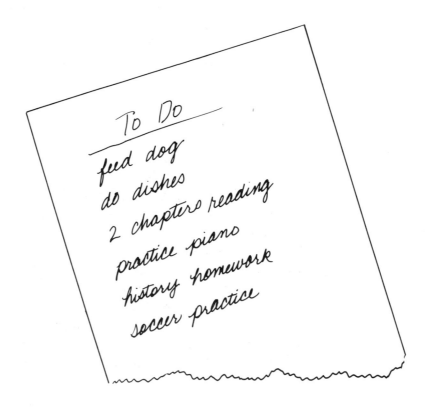

Activity 1–9
Sizing Up Your Instructor

"That instructor doesn't like me." "I can't do anything right in his class." "I never know what to expect in her class." Do you recall making similar remarks? If so, maybe you never ask yourself what your *instructor* expects.

Teachers are as different from one another as you are from your friends. Some are very relaxed in their approach while others rely on lots of structure. Some are very explicit in what they expect from students and what kinds of tests they give. Others may not be so direct.

If you want to learn as much as you can and have the best possible grades, it's your job as a student to understand the expectations of each of your instructors. This process doesn't take long, and it's not difficult either. Use your powers of observation, and if you still aren't sure, *ask* your instructor.

To begin, in the first days of class spend a few minutes thinking about your instructor's expectations regarding the following: your behavior, participation, and note taking; his or her method of grading and testing; and, finally, the appropriate techniques you can use to study for that instructor's class. You will be amazed at the results! Not only will you know how to tailor your studying to each class and its instructor's expectations, you'll earn better grades and waste less time.

Next, select the instructor or class that you find most difficult. Remember, the purpose of this exercise is to guide you through an evaluation of your instructor's expectations about you as a student. Once you determine what those expectations are, you can adjust your efforts accordingly and thus minimize your study time and improve your grade.

On a separate sheet of paper, list the expectations of your instructor, as you understand them, in each of the following areas. Be sure to allow enough room to write.

Instructor's Expectations of My Behavior and Participation:
1. At the beginning of the hour;

2. During the hour;

3. At the end of the hour;

4. In general.

Instructor's Expectations in the Areas of:
1. Note taking;

2. Study techniques;

3. Tests;

4. Grades.

Activity 1-10
Accuracy of Instructor's Expectations

Take your list of perceived expectations (Activity 1–9) to the instructor you selected and ask him or her to read it to see just how accurate you were.

If you were good at predicting what your instructor wants, you're off to a strong start in his or her class. If, on the other hand, you don't yet have a very clear picture of what is expected, ask your instructor specific questions about each area on your expectations list until you understand what he or she wants. Learn now—not after a test. Surprises aren't fun when grades are involved.

```
S        Q        3    R
u        u             ___
r        e             Read
v        s
e        t
y        i             Recite
         o
         n             Review
```

Activity 1-11
The SQ3R Method

An important part of improving your study skills is finding a dependable study technique. Some of you may already have discovered a method that gives you good results, but others may have no system at all . . . and have grades that show it. If you haven't had the opportunity to develop a study technique yet, the SQ3R method may be for you.* On a separate sheet of paper, add notes on SQ3R to your Study Skills information.

SQ3R

As students, most of you know it is not enough to simply read an assignment. The act of reading does not insure that you will remember what you have read. Perhaps you daydream while you read, or maybe you are surrounded by background noise, commotion, or interruptions. In any case, you can't recall a thing about what you just read. Sound familiar?

You need to be an active participant as you read and study. You can do that by practicing a technique that involves you in the learning process—SQ3R. Many of you already use part of the SQ3R technique if you preview material. You carry it even further if, as you read, you try to find answers to questions about the materials. Both the previewing and questioning techniques are important steps in SQ3R, but there is more to it.

* SQ3R was developed in 1941 by Francis Robinson; it has become a popular and successful study technique.

S = Survey

The S in SQ3R stands for *survey* (or preview). This should already be a familiar term to you. To review, the steps in the survey are simple and take very little time. They are:

1. Look at the title;

2. Read the first paragraph or introduction;

3. Read the first sentence of each of the other paragraphs;

4. Read the last paragraph or conclusion.

The survey step helps you in four ways:

1. You get a glimpse of the contents of the material without having to read every word;

2. You get a feel for your familiarity with the material;

3. You can estimate the amount of time you should set aside for covering the material; and

4. You may actually double your comprehension when you do read the entire selection.

The survey does all this in a matter of minutes!

Q = Question

In order to become actively involved in the actual reading process, you need to read with a purpose in mind. That is, you need to *read to answer questions*. Look to the following sources for questions you can answer as you read:

1. Questions listed at the end of the chapter;

2. Questions provided by your instructor;

3. Headings you turn into questions; and

4. Questions on worksheets, quizzes, or tests.

Knowing the questions *before* you actually read the selection helps you read for a purpose. You will be an involved reader, and your comprehension and retention of the material will be greatly improved. Better yet, after you finish reading the selection, you will find you know the *answers* to the questions you had as you read.

R = Read

Try it. Read the material as an active reader with the goal of answering questions as you go along. You'll be surprised at how much more you'll get out of your reading assignment, and you'll feel good when your reading reveals answers.

Reciting after reading increases your retention of material.

R = Recite

The next step is to *recite* the answers to your questions. Recite aloud to another person or quietly to yourself what you have read. Studies show that students tend to forget as much as 80 percent of what they have learned from reading within two weeks after studying. But when students recited immediately after reading, they forgot only 20 percent during the same time period.

Recite it, and then write it down, if necessary. This is the proof that you understand and comprehend what you have read—that you have been actively involved in the reading process. You know what you have read because you can recite the answers to questions.

R = Review

After a few hours, or even a couple of days, *review* the answers to your questions. This step will keep the material fresh in your mind, and you can retain it and recall it accurately for longer periods of time.

In addition, using the SQ3R method will save you from test anxiety and late-night or all-night crash study sessions, cramming for exams. SQ3R helps you learn and retain the material so you can approach a test with confidence.

Activity 1-12
Practice with SQ3R

Learning anything that is new takes some practice before it feels comfortable; the SQ3R technique for studying is no exception. Start by trying the SQ3R method on a chapter from a textbook that is difficult for you. Use your notes and *think* about what you are doing and why you are doing it.

Next, give yourself a long-term trial with SQ3R. Commit to consciously using this technique for two weeks as you study *one* subject that gives you difficulty. Be conscientious and follow the procedure steps exactly. SQ3R is used successfully by many students—see if it is a technique that will work for you.

Activity 1–13
Unit Review

This is a review of what you have learned in Unit 1 on developing study skills. Try to remember the major points that were covered. On a separate sheet of paper, answer the following questions.

I.   Multiple-Choice
Number your paper from one to five. Place the letter of the correct answer beside the corresponding number.

1. In what order should you study subjects?

   A. Hardest or least interesting to easiest or most interesting
   B. Alternate types of activities
   C. First things first, in order of descending importance
   D. Any of the above

2. What is the benefit of a study budget or time sheet?

   A. Sets immediate goals
   B. Helps concentration because you are working against the clock
   C. Helps resist distractions
   D. All of the above

3. How long should a break be?

   A. Five minutes
   B. Ten minutes
   C. Fifteen minutes
   D. As long as you need it to be

4. What did the article you read say about taking breaks?

   A. They are optional and not really important.
   B. They are a waste of time and should be omitted.
   C. They are absolutely essential, or your concentration will falter.
   D. They should be taken frequently; every thirty minutes is best.

5. Your study schedule should be:

   A. Very rigid. If you do not follow it carefully you'll never develop any self-discipline.
   B. Flexible. You'll become frustrated and easily discouraged if it is too rigid and you can't live up to it.
   C. Quickly disposed of. A study schedule forces you to be too organized and has very little benefit.
   D. Made out for weeks in advance. Careful planning never hurt anyone.

II. Listing

6 to 12. Number your paper from six through twelve. Read the questions carefully, choose **one** of the two questions, and write the correct answers.

A. List seven tips concerning the setting or environment in which you should study if you wish to get maximum comprehension.
B. List the seven steps in previewing your text.

13 to 17. List the words represented by the name SQ3R.

III. Short Essay

18. Choose one of the following topics and write your answer in paragraph form.

A. Describe what is involved in previewing your text and discuss the benefits you found when you previewed three of your texts.
B. Discuss the value of creating a good study setting, explain the changes you made in your study setting, and conclude by discussing how these changes have helped you improve your concentration.
C. Explain the steps in SQ3R and discuss how this technique will be beneficial to you.

UNIT TWO

Note Taking

NOTE (nōt) n. Written record or communication

TAKE (tāk) v. To write down

lmost anyone would agree: Note taking can be a real chore! Some instructors talk so fast, you can't begin to keep up. Others wander from one subject to the next until you can't even remember the points they are trying to make. A fast talker leaves your hand numb from writer's cramp. A disorganized speaker leaves you dizzy with confusion—and with few notes in your notebook. You need a better, more efficient method for taking notes.

Notes and note taking are personal. No two students take notes in the same way, although each is trying to pick out the same main points from a lecture. Whether you consider yourself a skilled or unskilled note taker, your note taking can improve. You can learn to be more flexible and concise.

Unit 2 will give you experience using several methods of taking notes, as well as some shortcuts you can use—regardless of the type of note-taking technique you favor. The exercises in this unit will help you "streamline" your note taking; in other words, they'll help you develop skills that will make it easier to take notes efficiently. And, because you will soon be an efficient note taker, the notes you take will be more useful to you, too.

Activity 2–1
Evaluating Your Present System

This activity lets you evaluate your own note-taking techniques and illustrates a concise method for taking notes in the future. For those of you who have trouble deciding what to include in your notes, practice picking out the main points and subpoints from the material.

Part One

First, read the following selection entitled "Evaluating Your Present System." As you read, use your standard note-taking technique to take notes on a separate sheet of paper. When you finish, compare your notes with those in the answer key at the end of this book.

Evaluating Your Present System

Lectures given by teachers are fleeting things. The ideas and concepts presented, unless captured on paper by students taking notes, are quickly confused or forgotten. In order to recall a lecture's main points, you must develop good note-taking skills.

First, you have to concentrate on the lecture. You cannot think about your plans for the evening, tomorrow's dance, or your next car repair. Next, you must learn to pick out the speaker's important points and to exclude the insignificant details. To do this, listen for signal words. Third, you should develop a system for taking notes. Many students use an outline form because it is simple and straightforward. Fourth, you need to find ways to streamline your note-taking system. That is, don't miss an important point because you fall behind as you write. Last, you need to review your notes soon after taking them to fill in any additional information and refresh your memory on the major points.

Part Two

Compare the notes you took with the outline provided in the answer key at the end of this unit. How did you do?

1.   Did you use complete sentences? Complete sentences are a waste of time. Be brief, using only key words.

2.   Did you use an outline form, or any form at all? Would you describe your notes as clear or confusing?

3.   Did you capture the main point and all the subpoints? Signal words in this selection such as "First, . . . next, . . . third, . . . fourth, . . . and last" should help you recognize the subpoints.

4.   Did you use any abbreviations or shortcuts while taking your notes? If not, you'll want to focus on streamlining your note taking.

Activity 2–2
Note-taking Questionnaire

This activity uses a survey to give you insight into your thoughts about note taking, your individual note-taking practices, and your weaker areas in note taking. Take a minute to complete the survey that follows. Your responses will help you gain the most from this unit by emphasizing specific goals for you.

On a separate sheet of paper, number from one to ten. Leave enough room to make comments for each question.

Note-taking Questionnaire

1. When do you take notes? In class? While studying?

2. Do you find it difficult to take notes while studying? If so, why?

3. Do you ever borrow notes from someone else? If so, are they easier or harder to use than your own?

4. Do you find it difficult to take notes in class? If so, why?

5. Do you write complete sentences when you take notes?

6. List your instructors who expect you to take notes.

7. Do you take notes in those instructors' classes?

8. Do you have trouble picking out main ideas from material?

9. Do you use any shortcuts in taking notes? If so, what are they?

10. Do you feel that taking notes or not taking notes affects the grade you earn?

No two students take notes in the same way. What's important is to find the method that works best for you.

Activity 2-3
Outlining

The first note-taking technique presented in this unit is outlining, the most widely used method of taking notes. Outlining provides you with a well-organized set of notes to study from because it forces you to seek out the main idea and to recognize supporting details. You eliminate other unnecessary information. Once mastered, outlining can be a valuable tool for making you a better student.

Activity 2-3 introduces you to the basics of outlining. It focuses on recognizing main ideas from paragraphs and writing them in proper outline form. Once you have completed this activity, you will have a good understanding of what outlining involves.

If you are not new to outlining, sharpen your skills by reviewing the technique. To help you practice, your instructor may want to provide additional exercises.

Number from one to seven on a separate sheet of paper, leaving room for your comments. Read "The Basics of Outlining" as you follow these directions carefully:

1. Read the first two paragraphs in the article.

2. Answer Questions 1 to 4.

3. Read the next paragraph.

4. Answer Questions 5 to 6.

5. Read the following two paragraphs.

6. Answer Question 7.

7. Read the remainder of the selection and compare your answers to those at the end of this book.

The Basics of Outlining

```
I. Topic Sentence
  A. Major Point
    1. Subpoint
      a. detail
```

One of the most important skills for you to develop early in your school career is that of taking notes in an organized manner. In many classes note taking is required. Learning to take organized notes is essential because information is more easily remembered if it is structured when written down.

One of the first steps toward developing an organized note-taking system is being able to recognize the author's main idea; that is, you must clearly understand the point or central thought the author is communicating. That main idea is the topic sentence, and all the other sentences in the paragraph help to support it.

---

1. In Paragraph One, what is the main idea or topic sentence?

2. Where in the paragraph is the main idea or topic sentence located?

3. Find the main idea or topic sentence in Paragraph Two.

4. Where is it located?

You will discover that a paragraph's main idea or topic sentence may be found in a number of different positions in the paragraph. Most frequently, it is the first sentence of the paragraph; the author wants to begin with his or her main idea and use all the other sentences to develop that main idea. The second most frequent location for the topic sentence is the last sentence of the paragraph. By placing the main idea at the end, the author can present a number of details first and then tie them together or sum them up with the topic sentence. Sometimes the main idea may be stated in the first sentence and restated in the last sentence. And occasionally, the main idea may be sandwiched somewhere between the first and last sentences, or split between two sentences. Finally, the topic sentence may be missing altogether! Obviously, topic sentences that are the first or last sentences of a paragraph will be easiest to find. Locating those floating in the middle of a paragraph or split between sentences takes practice.

---

5. On your paper set up the outline form shown below:

   I.

      A.
      B.
      C.
      D.
      E.
      F.

   What is the main idea or topic sentence in the previous paragraph? Write it beside Roman numeral I.

6. What are the six major points in the previous paragraph? Using the capital letters A through F, list each one.

One of the most widely used methods of note taking—the outline—is preferred by many students because its format follows a specific structure and is concise. Notes taken in this manner are well organized and easily remembered.

---

7. On a separate sheet of paper, copy the outline form shown below:

I.

  A.
  B.
  C.
  D.

Write the main idea for the previous paragraph beside Roman numeral I and the major points beside the capital letters A through D.

Because outlines have specific structures, as mentioned above, you'll find outlining an easy technique to learn. Always write the main idea or topic sentence of a paragraph beside a Roman numeral. Then list each of the major points—those that provide information about the topic—beside a capital letter. Subpoints describe the major points and are listed beside numbers. Finally, supporting details that define, explain, give examples of, give proofs of, or give opinions about the subtopics are placed next to lowercase letters. The paragraph's ideas are thus placed in order of importance. Look at the following example:

I. Main idea or topic sentence

  A. Major points providing information about the topic

    1. Subpoints that describe the major points

      a. Supporting details for the subpoints

Now check your answers for questions one through seven with the answers given at the end of this unit. How accurate are your outlines?

Activity 2–4
More Practice with Outlining

Now that you are familiar with outlining, try your hand at outlining the main ideas and major points in "Paragraph One" and "Paragraph Two."

As you read "Paragraph One" and "Paragraph Two," take notes on a separate sheet of paper keeping in mind three goals as you write:

1. Your notes should be clear and concise.

2. Your notes should include the paragraphs' main ideas and major points.

3. Your notes should use shortcuts, like abbreviations, technical symbols, and personal shorthand.

Take steps to keep your mind from wandering. Don't sit in one position too long—from time to time, stretch to stay alert.

Paragraph One

There are three reasons for learning to take good notes. First, note taking helps you pay attention. While you are writing, you are concentrating, and your mind wanders less. You stay with the subject. Second, note taking helps you remember. In their book *Note Taking Made Easy*, Judi Kesselman-Turkel and Franklynn Peterson state that note taking is a muscle activity, and that our muscles "remember" better than our heads. They give as an example a sixty-eight-year-old man who climbed on a bike for the first time in forty years and, after a few shaky starts, was able to ride off down to the corner. Third, note taking helps you organize ideas. You learn to sort out and write down the main points and subpoints in an organized fashion.

Paragraph Two

In order to keep your mind from wandering when taking notes, there are several steps you can take. First, you can choose your seat carefully. Sit in one of the first few rows, away from distracting doorways and windows. Next, avoid friends, especially friends who capture your attention when you should be listening. In addition, avoid thinking of personal matters. Keep your thoughts on what the speaker is saying and not on your affairs outside of class. Last, stay awake and alert. Take your coat or sweater off if you're too warm, and sit up, with your pen held ready to write. You need to be an active listener.

Now compare your notes with the answers at the end of this book. How well do your notes match those outlines?

Activity 2–5
Signal Words

In this activity, you will continue to improve your note-taking skill and efficiency. Begin by reviewing your outlines from Activities 2–1, 2–3, and 2–4, and add three new note-taking terms to your vocabulary: *signal-words*, *full signals*, and *half signals*.

Signal words are extremely helpful tools for picking out important details. They serve as flags to indicate main points in sentences or paragraphs. There are two types of signal words: full signals and half signals.

Full signals are obvious flags; they are words such as "the first, the second, the third . . . ."

Half signals are less obvious; they are words such as "the next, the last, in summary, therefore . . . ."

After writing these terms and their definitions in your notes, look back at "More Practice with Outlining" (Activity 2–4) and list on a separate sheet of paper the full signals used in "Paragraph One" and "Paragraph Two." Can you find any half signals? List them. Check your answers with those at the end of this book.

Activity 2–6
Patterning

In Activity 2–6 you will learn when and how to use the patterning method of note taking. You may discover that you are already using patterning to write flowcharts in your biology, math, or computer lab classes. Sometimes concepts are clearer and information is easier to remember when drawn as a picture rather than written as an outline. In addition, when it's time to review, simple diagrams are easy to understand.

On a separate sheet of paper, practice the patterning method of note taking by drawing three generations of your own family tree. Choose either your mother's side or your father's side of the family and by listing your grandparents' names at the top of your paper. Below their names, list the names of their children (your parent, aunts, and uncles). At the bottom of your family tree, add your own name, as well as the names of your brothers, sisters, and cousins. The basic shape of your three-generation family tree pattern will look like the one following, with variations, of course, based on the number of children in each generation.

———

———   ———   ———

———   ———   ———   ———   ———   ———

Can you think of any other classes besides the three previously mentioned in which it would be best for you to take notes using the patterning method?

Activity 2–7
Listing

In Activity 2–7, the focus is on listing, a third method of note taking that is extremely straightforward. Listing is an appropriate form of note taking for such classes as history, when dates and important events must be learned, or classes that involve a lot of vocabulary terms and definitions.

When you use this method in class, listen carefully as your instructor lectures, and then build your list. If your source of information is the text or other printed material rather than your instructor's lecture, read carefully and be guided by signal words and key phrases.

To give you practice, your instructor may read a paragraph in class, asking you to use listing to take notes. If he or she does not do this, set up your own notes by listing the important events coming up for you this week. Begin with a heading such as "Events" and follow with a numbered list.

Events
1.
2.
3.
4.

Were you aware that you really do use three methods for taking notes: outlining, patterning, and listing? Did you realize that different subjects require different note-taking techniques?

Outlining and listing are helpful techniques for taking notes from textbooks.

Activity 2–8
Margin Notes

In addition to outlining, patterning, and listing, you need to know another time-saving method for note taking. However, you can use this method *only* when you own your text or are allowed to write on the material on which you must take notes. If writing in the book or on the material itself is permitted, you can take *margin notes*.

When you use margin notes as your form of note taking, you write down key points in the margin of your book as you read. Margin notes are convenient, providing you with a sufficient set of notes for reviewing at test time.

To practice taking margin notes, choose a set of notes from one of your other classes. Notes from a history, geography, or literature class would work well, as would notes from any other class where the information is fairly detailed. In the margin of your notes, beside the major points, write one to four key words that identify those major points. Now try looking at your margin notes as cues and reciting the major points they represent. Do you see what an important review technique taking margin notes can be at exam time?

Activity 2–9
Highlighting

A fifth method of note taking is highlighting. A highlighter is a marking pen available where school supplies are sold. It allows you to highlight (draw a line over) any key words or phrases you wish to note or emphasize. The ink of the highlighter is light enough to read through.

As a note-taking technique, highlighting saves you writing time and emphasizes key information to review as you study for a test. The obvious disadvantage, of course, is that you must own your own book or other written material in order to use the method.

To practice highlighting, use the highlighter marking pen to draw a line through (or identify) the most important points in a set of your notes—the points your instructor might include on your next test. You'll probably agree it is much easier to study from a set of highlighted notes, than from notes in which every word seems to be as important as the next one.

Activity 2–10
Streamlining

Now that you have five methods of note taking to draw from, let's look at some methods of making note taking easier for you. Do you feel as if you are writing a book as you try to keep up with your instructor's lecture? If so, you need to learn some shortcuts—some ways to streamline your note taking.

As you read "Streamline Your Note Taking," take notes on each of the streamlining techniques. Then, to help you remember what you have read, illustrate each technique with at least three of your own examples.

Streamline Your Note Taking

When you think of streamlining your note taking, you probably think of taking shortcuts such as writing abbreviations in your notes whenever possible. Here are some abbreviations you may already be using:

subj. for *subject*   dept. for *department*

Nov. for *November*   assn. for *association*

But there are more ways you can streamline your note taking. Other practical techniques and examples are listed below:

1. **Leave periods off abbreviations.**
   ex for *example*   no for *number*
   st for *street*   dif for *different*

2. **Use common symbols.**
   & for *and*   + for *plus* or *positive*
   × for *times (multiplication)*   # for *number*

3. **Eliminate vowels.**
   If you are unfamiliar with conventional shorthand, the no-vowel system may save you when you have an instructor who has a very rapid speaking style. Try to read the following set of notes taken using the no-vowel technique:

   Ths prgrph ws wrttn n th "n vwl" nd th "bbrvtd" tchnq.
   Nt ll stdnts lk 2 tk nts ths wy, bt t wrks wll 4 sm. f y
   cn rd ths, y ndrstnd th mssg.

4. **Use word beginnings.**
   Many of you use this technique when you abbreviate.
   intro for *introduction*   com for *committee*
   info for *information*   rep for *representative*

5. **Add "s" to abbreviations to form plurals.**
   exs for *examples*   abbs for *abbreviations*
   mos for *months*   yrs for *years*

6. **Use personal shorthand.**
   Make up abbreviations that are meaningful to you. They need not make sense to other people; if you understand them and they save you time, they are valuable. Did you, for example, use *NT* anywhere in this unit instead of note taking?
   w/ for *with*   4 for *four* or *for*
   w/o for *without*   B4 for *before*

Activity 2–11
Unit Review

On a separate sheet of paper, complete the following to see if you can recall the major points presented in Unit 2.

I. True–False
Number your paper from one to ten. Write *true* if the statement is true; write *false* if the statement is false.

1. In order to take good notes, you must concentrate on your instructor's lecture. To do this, you might have to choose a seat away from friends.

2. It is important to review notes soon after taking them.

3. Good notes include all the important points, but they also include some unimportant points.

4. You should choose one system of note taking and stick to that; it is never necessary to use more than one system.

5. In taking notes, you look for the main ideas, which are the points the author is trying to make.

6. The main idea appears in only one position in the paragraph; you will always find it in the first sentence.

7. Note taking is a muscle activity; the muscles you use as you write help you remember the material.

8. Signal words may or may not help you in taking notes.

9. "First, second, third," and so on are called *half signals*.

10. To use margin notes or highlighting as your note-taking techniques, you have to own your textbook.

II. Five Methods of Note Taking
Number from eleven to fifteen. Briefly explain or illustrate with a drawing the five methods of note taking.

11. Outlining

12. Patterning

13. Listing

14. Taking margin notes

15. Highlighting

III. Listing
Number from sixteen to thirty. List five ways to streamline your note taking and give two examples of each.

16 to 18. First streamlining technique and two examples.

19 to 21. Second streamlining technique and two examples.

22 to 24. Third streamlining technique and two examples.

25 to 27. Fourth streamlining technique and two examples.

28 to 30. Fifth streamlining technique and two examples.

IV. Short Essay

31. Describe the method of note taking you find the most useful and explain why it is your preference.

32. Explain what you found to be the most valuable information in this unit and how knowing it will help you.

UNIT THREE

Taking Tests

TAKING (tāk′ing), v. To determine through measurement or observation

TEST (tĕst), n. A series of questions or problems designed to determine knowledge or comprehension

What words come into your mind when "tests" are mentioned? Success or failure? A's or F's? Do you grow numb with panic and dread the thought of a marathon study session late at night? Maybe you feel calm and confident and look forward to doing well. Think about your attitude toward taking tests.

As you already know, tests play an important part in determining your final grades in class. Because of this, it is essential that you know not only *how to study* for tests, but also *how to take* tests.

What *do* you know about preparing for and taking tests? Experts report that you have command of only 20 percent of the material when you cram the night before an exam, and that you will probably experience fatigue, loss of concentration, and test anxiety when you study that way. Do you cram or do you review briefly for several nights prior to the test?

Perhaps your difficulty is not with studying for the test, but with taking it. You become so nervous that you find it hard to concentrate on what you know. In this unit you'll find a list of simple techniques to help you eliminate test anxiety.

Once you study your notes and text and conquer your nervousness, all you have to do is sit down with the test and begin answering the questions, right? Not exactly. When you take a test, you show your instructor how much you know about the subject covered, of course. But you *also* show your instructor what you know about test-taking procedures. You may be surprised to learn that there are specific strategies for taking specific kinds of tests; for example, multiple-choice requires a different strategy from true–false.

Do you want to improve your test scores? Study carefully the information in this unit regarding preparing for tests, reducing test-taking anxiety, and taking tests. Your efforts here will earn you better test scores.

Activity 3–1
Memory

To learn how to study for tests, you need to learn the basic principles concerning how your memory works and why you cannot always remember material. It is frustrating to study for several hours the night before a test, only to find you don't remember several important things—even though you can sometimes remember the page they were on. Or, worse yet, you manage to remember those elusive things just as you hand in the test and leave the room.

There is a simple explanation for this, and it has to do with how your memory works. Start a section of notes entitled "Test Taking." Then read the selection entitled "How Your Memory Works." As you read, write down what goes on in each layer of memory.

How Your Memory Works

Test! Mention the word, and some people instantly feel fearful and tense. Yet, if you take time to prepare ahead for tests, you don't have to experience such stress.

In order to understand how to prepare for tests, it is helpful to know *how* you remember things. In *How to Study in High School,* Jean Snider describes the four memory layers in your brain.

Layer One

Layer One is for short-term memory. If a teacher gives you a definition and you can repeat it immediately, Layer One is at work. But if you are asked to give that definition the next day, chances are very good that you won't be able to remember it. Short-term memory is exactly that; it is useful for many daily, routine things such as making telephone calls or following directions immediately after they are given, but it is *not* useful for passing tests.

Layer Two

Layer Two is for slightly longer retention, Snider says. If your instructor announces a test will be given four days from now, and he or she repeats the announcement several times, the message goes from Layer One to Layer Two of memory. It is the *repetition of the information* that forces it from Layer One to Layer Two, yet Layer Two is still not very reliable. You will study the test material the night before the test. But during the test, some—if not many—of the answers will escape you.

When you spend the night before a test cramming and then can't remember the answers for the test—even though you can picture the page they were on—the explanation for your memory lapse is simple. The information you studied only went as far as Layer Two.

Layer Three

Layer Three offers good retention, providing you *repeat the information several times* and *write it down*. Your writing creates a visual image for your mind to remember.

Say, for example, your instructor provides you with terms and their definitions and you repeat them to yourself several times and write them down. You will have forced that information into Layer Three, and you should expect fairly good recall for the test.

Now you know why it is necessary to take notes on material you need to remember, why a written sample test that you construct prior to the real test is valuable, and why writing down key words as you review is beneficial. Your muscles help you remember as you write, and your memory sees the material on paper again and takes a picture of it.

Layer Four

Snider says the passage of time is a must for forcing material into the fourth layer of memory. You must *repeat* those definitions each night *over a period of time* and *write them down* in order for material to reach Layer Four. But once there, the material is locked in long-term storage.

Smart test takers start reviewing for a test at least three or four days before it will be given. Cramming the night before is not reliable learning. It won't give you the results you want.

Summary

Layer One: no repetition—short-term, unreliable memory.

Layer Two: some repetition—slightly longer retention, but not reliable.

Layer Three: repeating and writing down the information—fairly good retention.

Layer Four: repeating and writing down information over a period of three to six days—excellent retention.*

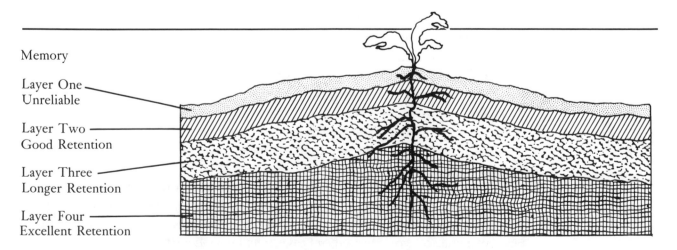

Memory

Layer One
Unreliable

Layer Two
Good Retention

Layer Three
Longer Retention

Layer Four
Excellent Retention

*Snider, Jean. *How to Study in High School.* Providence, RI: Jamestown Publishers, 1983, pp. 36–38.

Activity 3-2
How Do You Prepare for Tests?

Now that you know how your memory works, find out how you can organize your study time to suit your memory. In preparing for a test, do you reread the chapter the night before the test? Perhaps you review your notes or answer the questions at the end of the chapter. Have you ever tried to create a sample test for yourself or have someone quiz you?

Using a separate sheet of paper, make a list of the steps you take in preparing for an exam. List everything you do and when you do it. Then, if your instructor allows time, compare your list with your classmates' lists. Brainstorm as many different ways to prepare for tests as you can, and write down each of the methods on your sheet of paper.

If you are doing this exercise as an independent study, interview five successful students you know to find out how they prepare for exams. Or, interview five different instructors for their ideas on studying for tests. Whichever method you choose, be sure to include the results of your interviews in your notes. You will be sharing these results with your instructor.

Activity 3-3
How Should You Prepare for Tests?

You know how you prepare for tests, and now you know how your classmates go about it. How do your methods compare? Think about some of the new ideas or techniques for preparation that you learned from your peers. Based on what you know about their methods, can you see why one student scores well on tests, while another scores poorly?

The exercise should make this much clear: Rereading the entire chapter the night before a test is a waste of time. Your memory can't possibly absorb and retain all that material in one night. Instead, anticipate questions you think will be asked and review their answers three to six days in advance of the test date.

Now, compare your list of preparation techniques with the list that follows; add any suggestions your list did not include. When you finish, you will have a list of study techniques that, if you use them, will enable you to do well on *any* exam.

Preparing for Tests

1. Ask or anticipate *what material* will be covered on the test and write it down. You can do this by doing the following:

   Look at tests from other chapters and ask your instructor, or students who have taken the class before, what material might be included.

Listen to verbal clues in class. (Verbal clues are like signal words; they "flag" what your instructor considers to be important and may include on the test. Verbal clues are phrases such as "Be sure to remember that . . ."; "Take notes on this . . ."; "You may see this again . . . .")

Pay attention to what your instructor writes on the chalkboard. Write it in your notes and use your highlighter pen to emphasize it; there is a good chance questions relating to it will be on the test.

2. Find out what *type of questions* will be on the test.

   Use a different study technique for an essay test than for an objective test. Solving problems involves different preparation than sentence completion does.

   Look at past tests to discover your instructor's usual test format.

   Ask your instructor, or students who have had the class before, what types of questions will be included.

   Listen to lectures and class discussions for clues about the kinds of questions that might be included.

   Pay attention to the kinds of exercises you do daily in class; the test may parallel these.

3. Discover how much of the test is based on your notes.

   Consider your instructor's attitude about note taking—required or optional. It's a clue to whether he or she will test over notes.

   Talk to students who have had the class before, or ask your instructor if you will be tested over the notes.

   Analyze previous tests to determine the extent of test material drawn from notes.

4. Organize your notes and other study aids to correspond with the material you believe will be covered and the type of test to be given.

   Gather the material you feel might be on the test (notes, chapter review, problems, etc.).

   Highlight in your notes the key points that might be covered.

   Use margin notes (key words written in the margin) to identify main points.

   Write down any additional information you anticipate will be covered.

5. Avoid cramming. Keep in mind that it takes time to get material into the third and fourth layers of your memory, so begin reviewing the material three to six days prior to the test:

First night—skim the material.

Second night—skim the material, read margin notes, and recite important points aloud as you read them. (Those of you who learn best by hearing things should study that way, too. Hear yourself *say* the key points to be learned.)

Third night—read your margin notes (key words) and, without looking at your notes or the text, recite aloud the important points they represent.

Fourth night—make up a sample test and answer the questions, or have someone quiz you. If you do well, you do not need to study a fifth night. If you feel you need to do better, look over the material again and repeat this process a fifth, and perhaps a sixth, night.

6. Prepare yourself the night before the test.

Briefly review the material one more time (if you are a night person and do your best work at night).

Get adequate sleep.

7. Prepare yourself the next day.

Briefly review the material one more time when you wake up (if you are a morning person and do your best work during the morning).

Eat a nutritious breakfast (not donuts and coffee).

Get your mind and body stimulated with brief exercise (short jog, walk, push-ups) and a shower.

Wear something comfortable that makes you feel confident.

Get rid of test anxiety (see Activity 3–4).

Avoid drugs (drugs make you feel sluggish or nervous and affect your ability to recall and concentrate).

Build your self-confidence (tell yourself you have prepared well and so you will do well; a good attitude yields good results).

Exercise is a great way to reduce test anxiety.

Activity 3–4
Test Anxiety

There are just a few minutes to wait before your instructor puts a test in front of you. Are you feeling fidgety and tense, or even sick to your stomach?

If that describes how you feel before you take a test, you probably have test anxiety. Test anxiety is common for most everyone; even the best students have it. But, if you are to do well on a test, your test anxiety must be controlled. How can you control it? Practice some of the following tips.

Read the suggestions below and, on a separate sheet of paper, write down the tips you feel will be valuable for you. Not all of these suggestions work for everyone because people have different personalities. For some, thumbing through the book prior to an exam builds confidence and reassures them that they know the material. For others, it creates panic because they are afraid they may have forgotten to study something. Those people are better off leaving their textbooks at home. Consider each suggestion, then write down only those that will work for you.

Relieving Test Anxiety

1. Get enough sleep.

2. Eat a good meal prior to the test.

   Do not eat too much so that you feel groggy, but eat enough to provide your mind and body with the calories they need to function well.

   Greasy and acidic food and beverages (donuts and coffee) will not provide adequate nutrition and may upset your stomach.

3. Exercise to reduce tension and stimulate thinking.

   Exercise is a great stress reducer. Jogging, walking, mild aerobics, push-ups, and other forms of exercise will not only reduce test anxiety, but will stimulate your mind and body to improve your ability to think and concentrate as well.

4. Take a shower.

   Warm water relaxes some; cold water stimulates others.

5. Allow enough time to arrive at the class without hurrying.

   Hurrying causes tension; the fear of being late builds anxiety.

6. Provide yourself with time in the classroom to relax and compose yourself.

   Deep breathing exercises accomplish this. Take a deep breath, then another short breath, and exhale slowly.

   Close your eyes and imagine a relaxing scene. Allow your muscles to relax. Then think about your test while you are in this relaxed state.

7. Review with your friends *or* Don't review with your friends just prior to the test.

   For some, reviewing with friends before the exam builds confidence; it causes them to feel they have command of the material. For others, it incites panic; it makes them feel they don't know the material as well as they should.

8. Thumb through your books and notes *or* Don't thumb through your books and notes just prior to the test.

   Thumb through your notes if it builds confidence; don't look at your notes if doing so creates panic.

9. Develop a positive attitude.

   Tell yourself you studied as well as you could have for the test and *believe it*. Convince yourself that others have done well on this test, and you can, too.

10. Make sure you can see a clock, plan your time, and pace yourself.

   Not knowing how much of the test-taking time has elapsed creates anxiety. Budget your time, so you have time to answer all of the questions.

11. Choose your seat carefully.

   Sitting near friends can be disrupting. If you see them writing furiously, it can make you nervous. If you see them handing in their papers early, you may feel compelled to do the same, and your anxiety will build.

   Some people may read the test questions softly but audibly as they concentrate. Others may chew gum loudly. These are distractions that may annoy you and cause anxiety. Isolate yourself, if possible.

12. Begin by filling in the answers you know.

   This builds confidence and relieves anxiety because you see that you *do* know the answers. Also, it may trigger recall of other answers that you had momentarily forgotten.

13. Don't panic if others are busy writing and you are not.

   By spending time thinking, you may provide higher quality and better content answers than someone who is writing frantically.

14. Don't panic if you forget an answer.

   Go on to other questions—the answer will probably occur to you as you continue taking the test.

15. Don't worry if others finish before you do.

   Finishing first does not guarantee the best grade. Usually the better papers are handed in by the students who spent more time thinking about and checking over their answers before turning in their papers.

16. Don't panic if you run out of time.

   Ask your instructors if you can stay late; many will let you do this to finish.

Outline essay questions you didn't have time to complete. Most instructors will give some points for outlines because they can see you knew the answers, but didn't have time to write them in essay form.

Activity 3–5
Strategies for Taking Tests

Now that you know how to handle the pretest jitters, you need to consider what to do when that test is in your hands. If you are a person who gulps and says "Go for it," you are probably not getting the highest grades you could get. Instead, try using a few test-taking strategies.

The first one is simple: Read the directions on the test carefully *before* you begin writing. If you miss the words "Choose one of the following three essay questions," and you try to answer all three questions, you'll probably run out of time and give incomplete answers. There are fewer unpleasant surprises when you read the directions.

Perhaps you have been in this unfortunate situation: You are running out of test-taking time, and you still have to complete two essay questions. For the first time, you notice that they are worth twenty points each, and now you don't have enough time to give thorough answers.

Who needs to use test-taking strategies? We all do. Remember, you are not only being tested on the material, you are also being tested on how much you know about taking a test. So, to do the best you can on tests, you have to think about your own test-taking strategies. On a separate sheet of paper, list the steps or strategies you use when taking a test. After you finish, compare your list with your classmates' and, working as a class, develop a more comprehensive list. (If you are in an independent study, interview five successful students to compare your list with their lists of test-taking strategies, adding any new ones to your list.)

Now, compare your comprehensive list of test-taking strategies with the one below, and add to your list any techniques that you had not previously included.

Test-taking strategies help with tests on any subject.

Test-taking Strategies

1. Arrive early.

   Allow enough time to compose your thoughts, sharpen your concentration, organize your materials, and relax.

2. Bring all materials to class with you.

   Bring pencils or pens, paper, erasers, calculator (and extra batteries), and any other materials necessary for taking that test.

3. Listen carefully to your instructor's directions and comments.

   Instructors frequently announce changes in the test or emphasize instructions you may overlook; pay attention to what they have to say.

4. Look over the test, reading the directions carefully.

   If you don't answer the questions as instructed, you may lose points. Even an instruction as simple as "Write the complete word *true*" can cost you points if you don't follow it.

5. Budget your time.

   You should spend less time on a five-point completion than you spend on a twenty-point essay question.

   Determine the amount of time you have to take the test and the value and difficulty of each section. Then budget your time accordingly.

   If you have twenty questions and sixty minutes, spend three minutes per question; if you have four questions, each worth twenty-five points, and sixty minutes, spend fifteen minutes on each question.

   If you don't complete a question in the time you allotted, leave it and come back to complete your answer *only* if you have extra time.

6. Write down key facts or formulas in the margin.

   This is a safeguard against forgetting key information if you get nervous.

7. Look for qualifying words.

   Words such as *never, always, rarely, often, seldom, many,* and so on determine the correct answer.

8. Answer easy questions first.

   Answering the easy questions first will reduce anxiety, build confidence, trigger recall of other answers and the material you studied, and give you points immediately. You will be able to say to yourself, "This isn't so bad after all; I'm going to do well." And you'll approach the test with more vigor and confidence. Tackling the tough questions first may make you feel unprepared and uninformed, setting you up for failure.

9. Answer objective questions before essay questions.

   Completing the true–false, multiple-choice, and matching questions may provide you with answers to the essay questions.

10. If you don't know the answer, make a mark next to that question and try to complete it later.

    Often, answers you can't recall will occur to you as you take the test. If you have provided your memory with enough information, you will think of the answer. If not, don't panic—even the best students face this situation. Neatly write down the most suitable answer you can think of, and continue.

11. Guess at answers you don't know, unless there is a penalty for guessing.

    On true–false questions, you have a 50 percent chance of guessing right; on multiple-choice questions, you often have a 25 percent chance of being correct. Don't pass up potential points by leaving the question blank.

The only time you are penalized for guessing is when, in scoring the results, the number wrong is to be subtracted from the number correct. Not very many instructors use this technique, however. Most subtract the number wrong from the total possible.

12. Change answers *only* if you are sure they are wrong.

Most sources say first instincts are usually correct; however, sometimes you will recall information that will lead you to believe your first answer was incorrect. If so, make the change.

13. Use all the time allowed.

If you finish early, check your paper for errors.

Look again at the directions; did you follow them correctly?

Activity 3–6
Tricks for Taking Tests

Now you know that there are definite techniques for taking tests, and you have learned the best way to approach tests in general. You are ready for some details. There are specific tricks you can use to take a true–false test, or a multiple-choice test, or an essay test, for example. If you don't know these tricks, you are at a definite disadvantage, and your grades will reflect it.

To your notes on test taking, add a page labeled "Tricks for Taking Tests." List the following types of tests and, beneath each, write any tricks you already use when taking that kind of test. Leave plenty of space to add additional tricks in each section. The types of tests include: True–False, Multiple-Choice, Matching, Completion, and Essay.

Compare your list of tricks with those of your classmates, add to your list, and then compare your comprehensive list with the one that follows. If you are in an independent study, go directly to the following list and fill in the tricks you are missing.

Tests-taking Tricks

True–False
1. Beware of qualifying words.

Words such as *always, all, none, never,* and so on **usually** will make a statement false. Very few facts are absolute, and one exception to such a question will make it false.

Words such as *usually, sometimes, generally,* and *frequently* will **usually** make a statement true.

2. Look at the length of the statement.

    In order for a statement to be true, all parts of it must be true. The longer the statement, the more room there is for a false segment.

3. Be aware of false logic.

    Two statements that are true may be linked with a word that makes them false. Watch for that connecting word. For example: "The U.S. space shuttle program is famous because there was a shuttle crash." The shuttle program **is** famous and there **was** a shuttle crash, but the crash is not what made the program famous. The *because* makes the statement false.

4. Guess if you don't know the answer.

    You have a 50 percent chance of answering correctly, so take the chance.

Multiple-Choice

1. Eliminate the answer(s) that is (are) obviously incorrect first.

    Instructors usually structure a multiple-choice question with one statement that is obviously incorrect. Pick out that statement.

2. Read the question carefully.

    The question may say "Which is *not* an example of . . . ," "Which is the *incorrect* answer . . . ," or "Choose the *best* answer . . . ."

3. Read all the choices.

    You may believe that the first option is the correct one. Read the remaining options anyway. The most correct answer may be further down the list.

4. Pay attention to "all of the above" questions.

    "All of the above" is frequently the correct answer when it appears as a choice. To determine the extent of students' knowledge, instructors occasionally like to list several correct answers and conclude with "all of the above."

If two statements appear to be true, you are unsure about the third statement, and the fourth choice is "all of the above," the fourth choice is often correct.

5. Look for the longest answer.

The longest multiple-choice answer is frequently the correct one. The answer is carefully constructed to be complete.

Matching

1. Read the list on the right first.

First, read the list on the right, which contains the answer choices, so that you are aware of all the possibilities for answers.

Your instructor may have written one answer that appears to be correct near the top of the list, but a more correct answer may come lower in the list. If you do not read the entire list first, you will not know all the options.

2. If you are unsure of an answer, mark that question and return to it later.

Solve these by process of elimination after you have finished using the answers you are sure are correct.

Completion (Fill-in-the-Blank)

1. Reread the question several times.

Completion is popular with instructors because they can simply write down a statement and leave out a key word(s).

In rereading the question several times, the key word(s) omitted may, because of the repetition, suddenly occur to you.

2. Look for context clues.

Often, within a completion there are clues to the correct answer. If the blank you are to complete is at the end of the statement, you have more clues to use than if the blank falls at the beginning of the statement.

3. *A* and *an* are context clues.

    If *an* appears, the word following must begin with a vowel.

4. Look at the verb in the sentence.

    If it is singular, the subject or answer must be singular. If it is plural, the subject or answer must be plural.

5. Mark the statements you cannot complete and return to them.

    Recall of the information you need may be triggered by completing other statements.

Essay

1. Plan your time carefully.

    It is easy to lose track of time when writing an essay question response; budget your time and stick to your budget.

2. Know your facts.

    In objective tests, such as multiple-choice and matching, you have to select the correct answer from other choices given. In answering essay questions, you must frame your own answer, and to do it correctly, you must know the information needed.

3. Organize or outline your answers.

    In the margin, on the back of the paper, or in the space for the answer, write an outline first. List the facts and number them according to the order in which you wish to discuss them.

    Outlines enable you to present all the key information in an abbreviated, organized manner. You are less likely to omit important information or ramble in your answer if you outline first.

    If you have the key information in an outline, but run out of time in writing your essay, most instructors will give you partial credit for the outline. They can see you knew the information.

Answers presented in a helter-skelter fashion do not represent the logic, reasoning, and organization instructors look for in an essay answer. If your essay is not organized, you will probably lose points.

4. Understand the test terminology.

   Be certain that you understand what is being asked when the essay question instructs you to compare and/or contrast. *Evaluate* is different from *analyze* and *interpret* is different from *illustrate*. Activity 3–7 will give you some practice in reviewing these terms.

5. Write neatly, leave suitable margins, and provide space between answers.

   A good answer is not good at all if it is illegible. Most instructors penalize for sloppy work and look more favorably on work that is neatly done.

6. Write using complete sentences.

   Essays require complete sentences. Hurried thoughts scribbled in brief do not comply with the more formal essay structure.

7. Restate the question in the first sentence of your essay.

   Don't stumble around. Get right to the point. If the question is "Discuss the seven ways to improve your study setting," your answer should begin with "The first of the seven ways to improve my study setting involves . . . ."

   Your instructor will know you are going to be concise and logical and will begin with a favorable attitude toward your answer.

8. Use transition words to emphasize your organization.

   Tie your thoughts and concepts together with transitions such as the following: *for example, because, for this reason, however, likewise, in summary, ultimately.* There are many transition words you can choose.

9. Keep your answer simple and concise.

   Avoid flowery language that is meant to pad an answer with words but no information. Instructors can see through that.

10. Identify the favorite concepts of your instructor and use them.

   If your instructor is sure that TV has ruined the study habits of millions of students, and he or she seems to dwell on that concept, use it in your discussion if it applies.

11. Include a conclusion or summary.

   Restate your major points in your summary or conclusion. This step will reassure your instructor of your logic, organization, and key points.

Activity 3–7
Test Terminology

One of the main points mentioned previously involved knowing what type of answer was being asked for on an essay test. *Trace, discuss, justify, review, illustrate*—are you familiar with the subtle differences in test terminology? You can write a lengthy essay answer full of facts and logic, but if you did not address the question, you may score no points at all.

Consider the following terms typically found in essay exams. On a separate sheet of paper, list each term and an explanation of what is required when answering that type of essay question. If you don't know or are not sure what the term means, leave the space next to the term blank and fill in the correct answer later.

A. list	E. summarize	I. compare
B. outline	F. trace	J. contrast
C. define	G. describe	K. discuss
D. criticize	H. diagram	L. justify

How did you do? Sometimes just knowing what answers are suitable for particular terms found on essay tests can add points to your total score. Compare your list of terms and definitions with those found in the answer key at the end of this book. Correct any errors you made and add those answers you omitted. This list of terms should be added to your section of notes on Test Taking.

Activity 3–8
Reviewing Your Test

Let's assume you have prepared properly for an upcoming test, reduced the test anxiety successfully, followed the strategies you learned for taking tests, and applied the tricks for taking specific kinds of tests. Now you have the completed, corrected test in your hands.

Do you trash it? File it? Frame it? You should analyze it—not by quickly glancing through it, but by spending time studying it. To complete this unit on test taking successfully, you need to analyze the completed, corrected product and use the information to prepare for future exams.

What kind of questions did your instructor include?

What material did your instructor cover—textbook, lecture notes, exercises from class, or some combination?

What was your instructor looking for in your answers?

What were your strengths in answering the questions?

What were your weak areas?

What test-taking strategies do you need to use again next time?

What changes do you need to make?

Use a test that you have taken recently, either from this class or another, and analyze it. On a separate sheet of paper, using the test you have supplied, answer the questions from the list preceding this paragraph.

Analyzing a corrected test is an excellent way to discover your test-taking strengths and weaknesses.

Activity 3–9
Unit Review

On a separate sheet of paper, answer the following questions. Try to remember the main points and tips given in Unit 3.

I. True–False
Number from one to twenty. Write *true* if the statement is true and *false* if the statement is false.

   1. When studying, repetition (repeating things several times) is not necessary for remembering things.

   2. The passing of time is necessary for forcing material into your memory so that you can remember it for a long period of time.

   3. You must repeat material several times *and* write it down in order to remember things well; it is not enough to simply repeat it.

   4. It takes approximately three to six nights prior to an essay test for proper review of the material.

   5. It takes only one night prior to an objective test for proper review of the material since objective tests are somewhat easier.

   6. It is always enough preparation when studying for a test to review your notes and go over chapter headings.

   7. Wearing something that makes them feel comfortable and confident helps some people do better on exams.

   8. It is helpful when beginning a test to write down important facts or a formula you might otherwise forget as you take the test.

   9. Answer the easy questions last and tackle the hard questions first. They are usually worth more points and you need to be sure you complete them.

10. Answer the essay questions before the objective questions. They are usually worth more points and you need to be sure you complete them.

11. When answering essay questions, outline your responses first, but do not write the outline down on your test paper.

12. Before beginning a test, budget your time. You should spend about the same amount of time on each question.

13. On true–false questions, you should generally choose the answer that was your first instinct. It is usually correct.

14. On multiple-choice tests you can usually eliminate one answer as being incorrect.

15. When taking a matching test, read the left-hand column first and then choose the correct answer from the right-hand column.

16. You should not guess on fill-in-the-blank questions.

17. You can reduce test-taking stress by doing deep-breathing exercises.

18. Some people reduce test-taking stress by thumbing through their textbooks just prior to exam time.

19. For many people, coffee and a donut are all they need for breakfast, even on the morning of a test day.

20. Exercise not only reduces stress, it also stimulates thinking.

II. Matching
Number from twenty-one to thirty. Match the following descriptions with the test terminologies they describe.

21. Give differences only.

22. Give meanings but no details.

23. Give details, progress, or history from beginning to end.

24. Prove or give reasons.

25. Provide a numbered list.

26. Give details or a verbal picture.

27. Give reasons pro and con with details.

28. Give both similarities and differences.

29. Give a series of main ideas supported by secondary ideas.

30. Give your own judgment or opinion based on reasons.

A. list

B. outline

C. define

D. criticize

E. trace

F. describe

G. compare

H. contrast

I. discuss

J. justify

K. summarize

III. Listing
Number from thirty-one to thirty-seven, and list seven steps in preparing for a test.

IV. Essay
Choose *one* of the following essay questions and answer it using the essay format discussed in Unit 3.

A. Discuss test anxiety. Begin by defining it and then describe ways that you can control it. (First identify controls that work for you, and then identify additional controls that may work for someone else.)

B. Describe the steps in taking a test. Include as many steps as you can.

C. Discuss the four layers of memory. Include the function of each layer, how you get information into that layer, and which layer you should use for test-taking preparation.

Using the Dictionary

USING (yōōz′ ing) v. to put into service

DICTIONARY (dĭk′ shə-nĕr′ ē) n. a reference book containing an alphabetical list of words and their meanings

ictionaries contain a lot of information. You may know that a dictionary can help you spell and find the meanings of unfamiliar words. But what you may not know is that a dictionary can also help you find words that have similar meanings, give you the population of Mankato, Minnesota, and tell you when the expression "last straw" was first used to refer to something other than the one that broke the camel's back. Information that you may have felt you needed to use an encyclopedia to find might instead be found in your dictionary.

Knowing how to use a dictionary is a valuable study skill. Once you learn how to find the information you need quickly, you can improve both your reading and writing skills.

Activity 4–1
Alphabetical Order

Not all dictionaries are alike. The dictionary you use at school may be different from the one you use at home or in the library. But one thing all dictionaries have in common is their basic organization; words are arranged in alphabetical order. So, to find a word in a dictionary—*any* dictionary—you need to know the order of letters in the alphabet.

Why should you improve your alphabetizing skills? Alphabetizing skills are especially useful when you are using a dictionary; however, they are also helpful when you want to find a section in the Sunday paper, locate a book in a library card catalog, or find a file in an office drawer.

Follow the instructions for each step of Activity 4–1. Try to increase your speed as you work through each section.

Section One

Using a separate sheet of paper, number from one to ten. Next to the corresponding number write the letters that come right before and right after the letter that is shown. For instance, in the first example using the letter *w*, *v* comes before *w* in the alphabet, and *x* comes after *w*.

1. __v__ w __x__   6. ____ s ____

2. ____ b ____   7. ____ g ____

3. ____ x ____   8. ____ c ____

4. ____ m ____   9. ____ l ____

5. ____ j ____   10. ____ q ____

Section Two

Using a separate sheet of paper, number from one to twelve. This time supply the missing letter in each group of letters. The first has been done as an example.

1. b __c__ d   7. w ____ y

2. v ____ x   8. e ____ g

3. j ____ l   9. t ____ v

4. q ____ s   10. m ____ o

5. a ____ c   11. f ____ h

6. i ____ k   12. g ____ i

Dictionaries are valuable tools for building reading and writing skills.

Section Three

Using a separate sheet of paper, number from one to ten. In the groups of letters below, the letters are scrambled. Write the one letter that should come *first* in each group beside the example.

1. b   f   g   (a)
2. m   p   z   l
3. r   x   c   g
4. q   s   v   y
5. w   t   m   p

6. l   f   s   k
7. t   s   r   x
8. l   p   d   q
9. h   e   k   i
10. i   m   k   q

Activity 4–2

Alphabetical Order

Using a separate sheet of paper, number from one to ten. Write the words in each group below as they would appear in alphabetical order. Note that each set of words begins with the same letter. You will have to look to the second or third letter to arrange these words. Use the first set as an example.

1. easy
   easement
   east

   Answer:
   easement, east, easy

2. grand
   garage
   garbage

3. locomotive
   locomotion
   location

4. shield
   shelter
   sheet

5. clank
   clangor
   clang

6. twilight
   twinkle
   twist

7. wood
   waste
   wonder

8. indent
   incident
   indicator

9. atomic
   atrocious
   attach

10. upstairs
    upstart
    upstage

Activity 4–3

Dictionary Terms and Definitions

Most people think of a dictionary only as a source of word meanings or spellings. Activity 4–3 gives you an opportunity to find other kinds of information in each dictionary entry. For example, do you know where the inflected form of a word is found? Or its variant spelling? What about the word's etymology? Are these all new terms to you?

The following illustration shows where in a typical dictionary entry to find such information. Remember that a page from your own dictionary may look slightly different from the page shown here; just check the beginning of your version for a section explaining how your dictionary is organized.

In the following illustration you'll notice various vocabulary terms—each serving as a label to identify some part of a dictionary entry. As you read on, you'll learn more about the meaning of these vocabulary terms and how your knowing and using them can sharpen your study skills.

Main entry

Inflected form(s)

Diacritical marks

Variant(s)

Pronunciation key

Guide words

Syllabication

Part of speech

Etymology

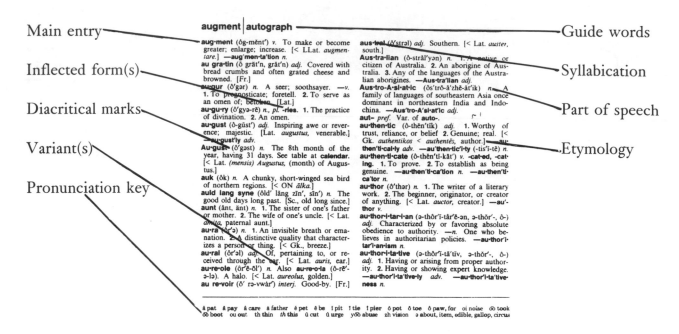

On a separate sheet of paper, take notes on the following dictionary terms and their definitions. Keep your notes brief.

Main Entry

The *main entry* is the word or phrase that you look up. It is usually printed in bold type in a position slightly to the left of the body of the entry.

Syllabication

The *syllabication* shows how a word is divided. The divisions are usually indicated by small dots. You can use syllabication when you write to determine how to divide a word at the end of a line. **Example:** goal • keep • er.

When you have to divide a word at the end of a line, you should follow the syllabication shown in your dictionary. However, also keep in mind these three rules:

1. Do not divide one-syllable words (house);

2. Do not divide a word so that only one letter is left on a line (able); and

3. Try to divide hyphenated words only at the hyphen (self-control).

Variants

Variants are two or more correct spellings of a single word. They are usually in bold type and may be treated in two ways:

1. If a variant spelling is separated from the main entry by the word *or* (or a comma in some dictionaries), that variant spelling is used as frequently as the spelling of the main entry. **Example:** *ax* or *axe (ax, axe)*. Both spellings, *ax* and *axe*, are used equally frequently.

2. If a variant spelling is separated from the main entry by *also,* the main entry spelling is preferred. **Example:** *medieval* also *mediaeval. Medieval* is the preferred spelling.

Etymology

A word's *etymology* indicates its origin (where it came from) and the etymological meaning of the word in that language. Etymologies usually appear in brackets or in parentheses. **Example:** the origin of the word retract is [< Lat. *retractare,* to handle again]. Etymologies may come directly after the main entry or, as in the sample dictionary page shown, at the end of the dictionary entry. A question mark in the etymology means that the origin of the word is unknown.

Inflected Forms

Inflections are changes in the form of a word due to a tense change or a plural form. To save space, dictionaries list only irregular inflected forms, such as the plural *oxen* for *ox* or the past tenses *swam* and *swum.* (If *ox* was regular, its plural would be *oxs,* and it would not be listed in the dictionary; if *swim* was regular, its past tense would be *swimmed,* and it would not be listed.)

Inflected forms usually appear in bold type following the label specifying part of speech. If inflected forms are not listed for a word, you can assume that these forms are regular.

You may want to look up inflected forms when you need to know any of the following information: the plural form of a word or how to spell it, or the past tense of a word or how to spell it. **Example:** *think* v. *thought, thinking.*

Parts of Speech

A word's *part of speech* is usually indicated by italic type (letters that slant) and often follows the main entry. It is important to check a word's part of speech to make sure that you do not use a word incorrectly. For example, when you see in the dictionary that a particular word is a noun, you won't try to use it as a verb. The part of speech is usually abbreviated. Some common abbreviations include the following:

n. — noun	*pron.* — pronoun
v. — verb	*conj.* — conjunction
adj. — adjective	*interj.* — interjection
adv. — adverb	

Homographs

Homographs are words that have the same spelling, but different meanings and origins. **Example:** *bark*—the noise a dog makes; *bark*—the outer covering of a tree; *bark*—a three-masted sailing ship.

Diacritical Marks

Diacritical marks are the dots, dashes, and other signs that show how to pronounce a word. The system for using these signs is usually explained in a *Pronunciation Key* at the top or bottom of the page. **Example:** potato (pə-tā′tō).

Guide Words

Guide words are the words at the top of the dictionary page. The guide words indicate the first and last main entry words found on that page. They help you to locate more quickly the word you want. **Example: broadcast / broth.**

Activity 4–4

Recognizing Dictionary Components

On a separate sheet of paper, number from one to nine. Use the following illustration to identify the numbered components of the dictionary entry. Choose the correct term from the list provided, and use each of the terms one time. Write the term beside the appropriate number on your paper.

main entry	pronunciation key	diacritical marks
etymology	part of speech	syllabication
guide words	variant	inflected forms

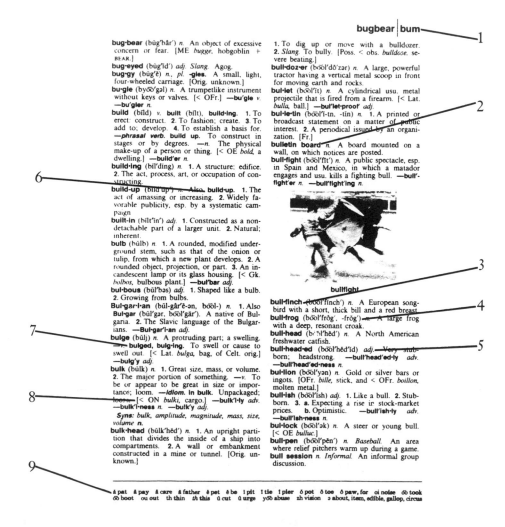

bugbear | bum ——————1

bug·bear (bŭg'bâr') *n.* An object of excessive concern or fear. [ME *bugge,* hobgoblin + BEAR.]
bug·eyed (bŭg'īd') *adj. Slang.* Agog.
bug·gy (bŭg'ē) *n., pl.* **-gies.** A small, light, four-wheeled carriage. [Orig. unknown.]
bu·gle (byōō'gəl) *n.* A trumpetlike instrument without keys or valves. [< OFr.] —**bu'gle** *v.* —**bu'gler** *n.*
build (bĭld) *v.* **built** (bĭlt), **build·ing.** 1. To erect; construct. 2. To fashion; create. 3. To add to; develop. 4. To establish a basis for. —*phrasal verb.* **build up.** To construct in stages or by degrees. —*n.* The physical make-up of a person or thing. [< OE *bold,* a dwelling.] —**build'er** *n.*
build·ing (bĭl'dĭng) *n.* 1. A structure; edifice. 2. The act, process, art, or occupation of constructing.
build-up (bĭld'ŭp') *n.* Also **build-up.** 1. The act of amassing or increasing. 2. Widely favorable publicity, esp. by a systematic campaign.
built-in (bĭlt'ĭn') *adj.* 1. Constructed as a non-detachable part of a larger unit. 2. Natural; inherent.
bulb (bŭlb) *n.* 1. A rounded, modified underground stem, such as that of the onion or tulip, from which a new plant develops. 2. A rounded object, projection, or part. 3. An incandescent lamp or its glass housing. [< Gk. *bolbos,* bulbous plant.] —**bul'bar** *adj.*
bul·bous (bŭl'bəs) *adj.* 1. Shaped like a bulb. 2. Growing from bulbs.
Bul·gar·i·an (bŭl-gâr'ē-ən, bōōl-) *n.* 1. Also **Bul·gar** (bŭl'gər, bōōl'gär'). A native of Bulgaria. 2. The Slavic language of the Bulgarians. —**Bul·gar'i·an** *adj.*
bulge (bŭlj) *n.* A protruding part; a swelling. —*v.* **bulged, bulg·ing.** To swell or cause to swell out. [< Lat. *bulga,* bag, of Celt. orig.] —**bulg'y** *adj.*
bulk (bŭlk) *n.* 1. Great size, mass, or volume. 2. The major portion of something. —*v.* To be or appear to be great in size or importance; loom. —*idiom.* **in bulk.** Unpackaged; loose. [< ON *bulki,* cargo.] —**bulk'i·ly** *adv.* —**bulk'i·ness** *n.* —**bulk'y** *adj.*
Syns: *bulk, amplitude, magnitude, mass, size, volume n.*
bulk·head (bŭlk'hĕd') *n.* 1. An upright partition that divides the inside of a ship into compartments. 2. A wall or embankment constructed in a mine or tunnel. [Orig. unknown.]

1. To dig up or move with a bulldozer. 2. *Slang.* To bully. [Poss. < obs. *bulldose,* severe beating.]
bull·doz·er (bōōl'dō'zər) *n.* A large, powerful tractor having a vertical metal scoop in front for moving earth and rocks.
bul·let (bōōl'ĭt) *n.* A cylindrical usu. metal projectile that is fired from a firearm. [< Lat. *bulla,* ball.] —**bul'let-proof** *adj.*
bul·le·tin (bōōl'ĭ-tn, -tĭn) *n.* 1. A printed or broadcast statement on a matter of public interest. 2. A periodical issued by an organization. [Fr.]
bulletin board *n.* A board mounted on a wall, on which notices are posted.
bull·fight (bōōl'fīt') *n.* A public spectacle, esp. in Spain and Mexico, in which a matador engages and usu. kills a fighting bull. —**bull'fight·er** *n.* —**bull'fight'ing** *n.*

bullfight

bull·finch (bōōl'fĭnch') *n.* A European songbird with a short, thick bill and a red breast.
bull·frog (bōōl'frôg', -frŏg') *n.* A large frog with a deep, resonant croak.
bull·head (bōōl'hĕd') *n.* A North American freshwater catfish.
bull·head·ed (bōōl'hĕd'ĭd) *adj.* Very stubborn; headstrong. —**bull'head'ed·ly** *adv.* —**bull'head'ed·ness** *n.*
bul·lion (bōōl'yən) *n.* Gold or silver bars or ingots. [OFr. *bille,* stick, and < OFr. *boillon,* molten metal.]
bull·ish (bōōl'ĭsh) *adj.* 1. Like a bull. 2. Stubborn. 3. **a.** Expecting a rise in stock-market prices. **b.** Optimistic. —**bull'ish·ly** *adv.* —**bull'ish·ness** *n.*
bul·lock (bōōl'ək) *n.* A steer or young bull. [< OE *bulluc.*]
bull·pen (bōōl'pĕn') *n. Baseball.* An area where relief pitchers warm up during a game.
bull session *n. Informal.* An informal group discussion.

——2
——3
——4
——5
6——
7——
8——
9——

ă pat ā pay â care ä father ĕ pet ē be ĭ pit ī tie î pier ŏ pot ō toe ô paw, for oi noise ŏŏ took ōō boot ou out th thin *th* this ŭ cut û urge yōō abuse zh vision ə about, item, edible, gallop, circus

Activity 4–5
Discovering Etymologies

English is a language that has borrowed words and phrases from many languages. Sometimes the etymology of a word can help you determine its meaning, as when the word comes from a common Latin or Greek root. Other times, the meaning of the word has changed so much that it has little relation to the foreign word it developed from. For these reasons, discovering a word's etymology and etymological meaning can be very interesting.

The following activity will give you practice in reading etymologies in dictionary entries. Be sure to follow the instructions for each step.

Begin by numbering a separate sheet of paper from one to seventeen. Using the dictionary entries provided, find the etymology for each of the words listed.

---

emporium | encumber

employing. **2.** The state of being employed. **3.** An activity or occupation.
em·po·ri·um (ĕm-pôr'ē-əm, -pōr'-) *n., pl.* **-ums** or **-po·ri·a** (-pôr'ē-ə, -pōr'-). A store carrying a wide variety of merchandise. [< Gk. *emporion*, market.]
em·pow·er (ĕm-pou'ər) *v.* To invest with legal power; authorize.
em·press (ĕm'prĭs) *n.* **1.** The female sovereign of an empire. **2.** The wife or widow of an emperor. [< OFr. *emperesse.*]
emp·ty (ĕmp'tē) *adj.* **-ti·er, -ti·est. 1.** Containing nothing. **2.** Having no occupants or inhabitants; unoccupied. **3.** Lacking purpose, substance, value, or effect. —*v.* **-tied, -ty·ing. 1.** To make or become empty. **2.** To discharge or flow: *a river that empties into a bay.* —*n., pl.* **-ties.** An empty container, esp. a bottle. [< OE *ǣmtig.*] —**emp'ti·ness** *n.*
emp·ty-hand·ed (ĕmp'tē-hăn'dĭd) *adj.* **1.** Bearing nothing in the hands. **2.** Having gained or accomplished nothing.
em·py·re·an (ĕm'pĭ-rē'ən) *n.* **1.** The highest reaches of heaven. **2.** The sky or firmament. [< Gk. *empurios*, fiery.]
e·mu (ē'myōō) *n.* A large, flightless Australian bird related to and resembling the ostrich. [Port. *ema*, flightless bird of South America.]
em·u·late (ĕm'yə-lāt') *v.* **-lat·ed, -lat·ing.** To strive to equal or excel, esp. through imitation. [Lat. *aemulari.*] —**em'u·la'tion** *n.*
e·mul·si·fy (ĭ-mŭl'sə-fī') *v.* **-fied, -fy·ing.** To make into or become an emulsion. —**e·mul'si·fi·ca'tion** *n.* —**e·mul'si·fi'er** *n.*
e·mul·sion (ĭ-mŭl'shən) *n.* **1.** A suspension of small globules of one liquid in a second liquid with which the first does not mix. **2.** A light-sensitive coating, usu. of silver halide grains in a thin gelatin layer, on photographic film, paper, or glass. [< Lat. *emulgēre*, to drain out.] —**e·mul'sive** *adj.*
en (ĕn) *n. Printing.* A unit of measure equal to half the width of an em.
en-[1] or **em-** *pref.* **1. a.** To put into or on: *enthrone.* **b.** To go into or on: *entrain.* **2.** To cover or provide with: *enrobe.* **3.** To cause to be: *endear.* **4.** Thoroughly. Used often as an intensive: *entangle.* [< Lat. *in,* in.]
en-[2] or **em-** *pref.* In; into; within: *empathy.* [< Gk.]
-en[1] *suff.* **1. a.** To cause to be: *cheapen.* **b.** To become: *redden.* **2. a.** To cause to have: *hearten.* **b.** To come to have: *lengthen.* [< OE *-nian.*]
-en[2] *suff.* Made of or resembling: *wooden.* [< OE.]
en·a·ble (ĕn-ā'bəl) *v.* **-bled, -bling. 1.** To provide with the means, knowledge, or opportunity; make possible. **2.** To give legal power, capacity, or sanction to.
en·act (ĕn-ăkt') *v.* **1.** To make (a bill) into a law. **2.** To act out, as on a stage. —**en·act'ment** *n.*
e·nam·el (ĭ-năm'əl) *n.* **1.** A vitreous, usu. opaque coating baked on metal, glass, or ceramic ware. **2.** A paint that dries to a hard, glossy surface. **3.** The hard substance that covers the exposed portion of a tooth. —*v.* **-eled, -eled, -el·ing** or **-el·ling.** To coat or decorate with enamel. [< AN *enamailler*, to put on enamel.] —**e·nam'el·ware** *n.*
en·am·or (ĭ-năm'ər) *v.* Also *chiefly Brit.* **en·am·our.** To inspire with love; captivate. [< OFr. *enamourer.*]

en bloc (äɴ blŏk') *adv.* All together; as a whole. [Fr.]
en·camp (ĕn-kămp') *v.* To set up or live in a camp. —**en·camp'ment** *n.*
en·cap·su·late (ĕn-kăp'sə-lāt') *v.* **-lat·ed, -lat·ing.** To encase or become encased in a capsule. —**en·cap'su·la'tion** *n.*
en·case (ĕn-kās') *v.* **-cased, -cas·ing.** To enclose in or as if in a case. —**en·case'ment** *n.*
-ence or **-ency** *suff.* Action, state, quality, or condition: *reference.* [< Lat. *-entia.*]
en·ceph·a·li·tis (ĕn-sĕf'ə-lī'tĭs) *n.* Inflammation of the brain. —**en·ceph'a·lit'ic** (-lĭt'ĭk) *adj.*
encephalo- or **encephal-** *pref.* The brain: *encephalitis.* [< Gk. *enkephalos,* in the head.]
en·ceph·a·lon (ĕn-sĕf'ə-lŏn') *n., pl.* **-la** (-lə). The brain of a vertebrate. [Gk. *enkephalon.*]
en·chain (ĕn-chān') *v.* To bind with or as if with chains; fetter.
en·chant (ĕn-chănt') *v.* **1.** To cast under a spell; bewitch. **2.** To delight completely; enrapture. [< Lat. *incantare.*] —**en·chant'er** *n.* —**en·chant'ment** *n.*
en·chi·la·da (ĕn'chə-lä'də) *n.* A rolled tortilla with a meat or cheese filling, served with a sauce spiced with chili. [Mex. Sp.]
en·ci·pher (ĕn-sī'fər) *v.* To put (a message) into cipher. —**en·ci'pher·ment** *n.*
en·cir·cle (ĕn-sûr'kəl) *v.* **-cled, -cling. 1.** To form a circle around; surround. **2.** To move or go around; make a circuit of. —**en·cir'cle·ment** *n.*
en·clave (ĕn'klāv', ŏn'-) *n.* A country or part of a country lying entirely within the boundaries of another. [< OFr. *enclaver,* to enclose.]
en·close (ĕn-klōz') *v.* **-closed, -clos·ing.** Also **in·close** (ĭn-). **1.** To surround on all sides; fence in. **2.** To include in the same container with a package or letter. [< Lat. *includere,* to include.] —**en·clo'sure** (-klō'zhər) *n.*
en·code (ĕn-kōd') *v.* **-cod·ed, -cod·ing.** To put (a message) into code. —**en·cod'er** *n.*
en·co·mi·um (ĕn-kō'mē-əm) *n., pl.* **-ums** or **-mi·a** (-mē-ə). Lofty praise; eulogy. [< Gk. *enkōmios,* of the victory procession.]
en·com·pass (ĕn-kŭm'pəs, -kŏm'-) *v.* **1.** To surround. **2.** To comprise or contain; include.
en·core (ŏn'kôr', -kōr') *n.* **1.** A demand by an audience for an additional performance. **2.** An additional performance in response to an audience's demand. —*v.* **-cored, -cor·ing.** To demand an encore of or from. [< Fr., again.]
en·coun·ter (ĕn-koun'tər) *n.* **1.** A casual or unexpected meeting. **2.** A hostile confrontation, as between enemies; clash. —*v.* **1.** To meet, esp. unexpectedly. **2.** To confront in battle. [< OFr. *encountre.*]
en·cour·age (ĕn-kûr'ĭj, -kŭr'-) *v.* **-aged, -ag·ing. 1.** To inspire with courage or confidence. **2.** To help bring about; foster. [< OFr. *encoragier.*] —**en·cour'age·ment** *n.* —**en·cour'ag·ing·ly** *adv.*
en·croach (ĕn-krōch') *v.* To intrude or infringe gradually upon the property or rights of another; trespass. [< OFr. *encrochier,* to seize.] —**en·croach'ment** *n.*
en·crust (ĕn-krŭst') *v.* Also **in·crust** (ĭn-). To cover or become covered with or as if with a crust. —**en·crus·ta'tion** (ĕn'krŭ-stā'shən) *n.*
en·cum·ber (ĕn-kŭm'bər) *v.* **1.** To weigh down excessively; burden. **2.** To hinder; impede. [< OFr. *encombrer,* to block up.] —**en·cum'brance** (-brəns) *n.*

Write the etymology out in full (do not use abbreviations), and, if it is given, write the etymological meaning for each word. (Etymological meanings are found with the etymologies in the square brackets.)

You will need to know these abbreviations:

Gk—Greek	*Port*—Portuguese	*Fr*—French
OFr—Old French	*Lat*—Latin	*Mex Sp*—Mexican Spanish
OE—Old English	*AN*—Anglo-Norman	

1. enchilada
2. emporium
3. enclave
4. encroach
5. emu

6. enclose
7. encore
8. enamel
9. empty
10. encumber

11 to 17. Now write all the words from the dictionary page shown that have Old French as their etymology.

Activity 4–6
Using Other Information in a Dictionary Entry

This activity gives you practice in using some of the other information that is given in a dictionary entry. This time, you will check word division and find inflected forms of words. Why are these skills worth practicing? Because, in order to spell and write words correctly, you must know how they are divided and how their forms vary.

On a separate sheet of paper, number from one to ten. Refer to the dictionary entry provided as you answer the questions listed in Section One and Section Two below.

Section One: Syllabication

Using the dictionary entries on the next page, look up the words listed, determine their proper division into syllables, and write the syllabicated words beside the correct number on your paper.

1. glacial
2. gladiator
3. glamour

4. gladiolus
5. glaciate

gird (gûrd) v. gird·ed or girt (gûrt), gird·ing. 1. To encircle with or as if with a belt or band. 2. To fasten with a belt. 3. To equip or prepare for action. [< OE gyrdan.]
gird·er (gûr'dər) n. A strong horizontal beam used as a main support in building.
gir·dle (gûr'dl) n. 1. A belt, sash, or band worn around the waist. 2. A supporting undergarment worn over the waist and hips. —v. -dled, -dling. To encircle with or as if with a belt. [< OE gyrdel.] —gir'dler n.
girl (gûrl) n. 1. A female child or young unmarried woman. 2. Informal. A woman. 3. A sweetheart. 4. A female servant. [ME girle.] —girl'hood n. —girl'ish adj. —girl'ish·ly adv. —girl'ish·ness n.
girl Friday n. A female assistant with a great variety of duties.
girl·friend (gûrl'frĕnd') n. Also girl friend. 1. A female friend. 2. Informal. A sweetheart or favored female companion of a man.
Girl Scout n. A member of the Girl Scouts, an organization for girls between 7 and 17 that stresses physical fitness, good character, and homemaking ability.
girt (gûrt) v. A p.t. & p.p. of gird.
girth (gûrth) n. 1. Size measured by encircling something; circumference. 2. A strap encircling an animal's body to secure a load or saddle. [< ON györdh.]
gist (jĭst) n. The central idea; essence. [< OFr., it lies.]
give (gĭv) v. gave (gāv), giv·en (gĭv'ən), giv·ing. 1. a. To make a present of: give flowers. b. To make gifts. c. To deliver in exchange or in recompense: give five dollars for the book. 2. To entrust to or place in the hands of: Give me the scissors. 3. To convey: Give him my

gla·cial (glā'shəl) adj. 1. Of, relating to, or derived from glaciers. 2. Often Glacial. Characterized or dominated by the existence of glaciers. 3. Extremely cold. [Lat. glacialis, icy.] —gla'cial·ly adv.
gla·ci·ate (glā'shē-āt', -sē-) v. -at·ed, -at·ing. 1. To subject to glacial action. 2. To freeze. [Lat. glaciare, to freeze.] —gla'ci·a'tion n.
gla·cier (glā'shər) n. A large mass of slowly moving ice, formed from compacted snow. [< Lat. glacies, ice.]
glad (glăd) adj. glad·der, glad·dest. 1. Feeling, showing, or giving joy and pleasure; happy. 2. Pleased; willing: glad to help. [< OE glæd.] —glad'ly adv. —glad'ness n.
Syns: glad, cheerful, cheery, festive, gay, joyful, joyous adj.
glad·den (glăd'n) v. To make or become glad.
glade (glād) n. An open space in a forest. [Perh. < GLAD, shining (obs).]
glad hand n. A hearty, effusive greeting. —glad'-hand' v.
glad·i·a·tor (glăd'ē-ā'tər) n. 1. A man trained to entertain the public by engaging in fights to the death in ancient Roman arenas. 2. A person who engages in a sensational struggle. [Lat.] —glad'i·a·to'ri·al (-ə-tôr'ē-əl, -tōr'-) adj.
glad·i·o·lus (glăd'ē-ō'ləs) n., pl. -li (-lī', -lē') or -lus·es. A widely cultivated plant with sword-shaped leaves and a spike of showy, variously colored flowers. [< Lat. gladius, sword.]
glad·some (glăd'səm) adj. Glad; joyful. —glad'some·ly adv. —glad'some·ness n.
glam·or·ize (glăm'ə-rīz') v. -ized, -iz·ing. Also glam·our·ize. To make glamorous. —glam'or·i·za'tion n. —glam'or·iz'er n.
glam·our (glăm'ər) n. Also glam·or. An air of

Section Two: Inflected Forms

Using the same group of dictionary entries (above), look up the following words and write their inflected forms beside the correct number on your answer sheet.

6. give

7. glaciate

8. glamorize

9. glad

10. gird

Activity 4–7
Using Diacritical Marks

You have come across a new word in your reading. Looking up the meaning of that new word is not enough to learn it. You must also know how to pronounce the word, so you can say it as well as write it. Diacritical marks help you learn a word's pronunciation. They are the focus of this activity.

Section One

On a separate sheet of paper, number from one to ten. Using the pronunciation key as a guide, determine the pronunciation of the words in the left-hand column. Then match the words with their correct definitions by placing the letter of the definition beside the corresponding number on your answer sheet.

1. glā′shər
2. ô-thĕn′tĭk
3. o′thər
4. ĕn-ăkt′
5. ĕn-klōz′
6. brōō-nĕt′
7. brou
8. ĕn-kûr′ĭj
9. jīst
10. ô-gəst′

A. to act out, as on a stage
B. having dark or brown hair
C. the writer of a literary work
D. to inspire with courage
E. to surround on all sides
F. the forehead
G. genuine, real
H. the central idea
I. the eighth month of the year
J. a large mass of slowly moving ice

Section Two

The joke written below belongs to the "oldies but goodies" category. Use the dictionary pronunciation key to decipher it. Then, on a separate sheet of paper, write the answers to the questions that follow it.

Door′ing ə foot′bol gam, wun uv thə pla′ərs had ə kup′əl uv fing′gərs bad′le smash′d. Thə tem dok′tər igzamin′d and dres′d thə hand.
"Dok′tər," ask′d thə pla′ər angk′shəs-le, "wil i be abəl too pla thə pe-an′o?"
"Surtn′le yoo wil," promis′d thə dok′tər.
"Yoo′r wun′dər-fəl, dok′tər," sed thə hap′e plaər. "I kood nev′ər pla thə pe-an′o bi-for′!"

1. What happened to the football player?

2. What did the doctor promise him?

3. Why was the football player so pleased?

Activity 4–8
Other Kinds of Information in a Dictionary

Besides information about words and their meanings, many dictionaries provide information about geographical places and famous people. In addition, some dictionaries give information about grammar, punctuation, correct form for writing letters, and how to footnote information. Dictionaries may also include illustrations, so you can see what different alphabets look like or how a disc brake is constructed.

Dictionaries present these "extra" kinds of information in one of two ways. Usually, some of the special information is given in sections at the front or the back of the dictionary. Lists of grammar rules usually will appear in a special section separate from the word entries.

A second way of presenting such information is to include it in the body of the dictionary, among the word entries. For example, names of famous people or geographical places may be mixed in among word entries in the body of one dictionary, or they may fall in separate sections at the back of another dictionary.

To find out where you can find various kinds of information in your own dictionary, you should preview it, just as you would preview a textbook. Look at the table of contents and the introductory material. Then leaf through the pages, from front to back. If your dictionary has cut-out alphabet guides, you may also find guides for biographical (people) and geographical (places) lists.

Activity 4–8 gives you a chance to explore your dictionary for different kinds of information. On a separate sheet of paper, number from one to ten. Use the dictionary entries provided to answer the questions that follow.

1. Who was James Buchanan?

2. What is the capital of Brazil?

3. Draw a picture of the configuration of a benzene ring.

4. What is the pattern of sound for an *I* in Morse Code?

5. What does the abbreviation *a.k.a.* stand for?

6. What does the abbreviation *ASAP* stand for?

7. What is the formula for benzoic acid?

8. What was Buffalo Bill's real name?

9. What does the dictionary say about Bunker Hill?

10. When was George Bush born?

Morse code

A	·—		V	···—
B	—···		W	·——
C	—·—·		X	—··—
D	—··		Y	—·——
E	·		Z	——··
F	··—·		Á	·—·—
G	——·		Ä	·—·—
H	····		É	··—··
I	··		Ñ	——·——
J	·———		Ö	———·
K	—·—		Ü	··——
L	·—··		1	·————
M	——		2	··———
N	—·		3	···——
O	———		4	····—
P	·——·		5	·····
Q	——·—		6	—····
R	·—·		7	——···
S	···		8	———··
T	—		9	————·
U	··—		0	—————
, (comma)	——··——			
. (period)	·—·—·—			
?	··——··			
;	—·—·—·			
:	———···			
/ (hyphen)	—····—			
- (hyphen)	—····—			
apostrophe	·————·			
parenthesis	—·——·—			
underline	··——·—			

Buchanan | Cartier

Bu·chan·an (byōō-kăn′ən, bə-). **James.** 1791–1868. 15th U.S. President (1857–61).

Buck (bŭk). **Pearl Sydenstricker.** 1892–1973. Amer. author.

Bud·dha (bōō′də, bood′ə). 563?–483? B.C. Indian philosopher; founder of Buddhism. —**Bud′dhist** *n. & adj.*

Buf·fa·lo Bill (bŭf′ə-lō′ bĭl′). William Frederick Cody.

Buf·fon (bü-fôn′), **Comte Georges Louis Leclerc de.** 1707–88. French naturalist.

Bu·kha·rin (bōō-ĸнä′rĭn), **Nikolai Ivanovich.** 1888–1938. Russian revolutionary.

Bur·ton (bûrt′n). **1. Robert.** 1577–1640. English clergyman and author. **2. Sir Richard Francis.** 1821–90. English Orientalist and adventurer.

Bush (bŏŏsh), **George Herbert Walker.** b. 1924. U.S. Vice President (since 1981).

But·ler (bŭt′lər), **Samuel.** 1835–1902. English novelist.

861

AK Alaska.
a.k.a. also known as.
AKC American Kennel Club.
AL 1. Alabama. **2.** American League. **3.** American Legion.

AK | bact.

art. 1. article. **2.** artillery.
arty. artillery.
As. Asia; Asian.
a/s airspeed.
ASAP also **asap** as soon as possible.

Bolivia | Byzantine Empire

829

Bra·zil (brə-zĭl′). Country of E South America. Cap. Brasília. Pop. 107,145,200. —**Bra·zil′ian** *adj. & n.*

Bra·zos (brăz′əs, brä′zəs). River of E Tex., flowing c. 950 mi (1,528 km) to the Gulf of Mexico.

Braz·za·ville (brăz′ə-vĭl′). Cap. of Congo, on the N bank of the Congo. Pop. 175,000.

Bre·men (brĕm′ən). City of N West Germany, on the Weser R. Pop. 556,128.

Bren·ner Pass (brĕn′ər). Alpine pass between S Austria and NE Italy.

Bre·scia (brĕ′shä). Industrial city of N central Italy. Pop. 212,265.

Brest (brĕst). Also **Brest Li·tovsk** (lə-tôfsk′, -tôvsk′). City of W European USSR. Pop. 186,000.

Bridge·port (brĭj′pôrt′, -pōrt′). Industrial city of SW Conn. Pop. 142,546.

Bridge·town (brĭj′toun′). Cap. of Barbados, E West Indies. Pop. 8,789.

Brigh·ton (brīt′n). Seaside resort of SE England, on the English Channel. Pop. 152,700.

Bun·ker Hill (bŭng′kər). Hill in Charlestown, Mass., near site of 1st major Revolutionary War battle (1775).

Bur·gun·dy (bûr′gən-dē). Region and former duchy and province of SE France. —**Burgun′dian** (bər-gŭn′dē-ən) *adj. & n.*

Bur·ling·ton (bûr′lĭng-tən). City of NW Vt., on Lake Champlain. Pop. 37,712.

Bur·ma (bûr′mə). Country of SE Asia on the E shore of the Bay of Bengal and the Andaman Sea. Cap. Rangoon. Pop. 31,512,000. —**Burmese** (bər-mēz′, -mēs′) or **Bur·man** *adj. & n.*

Burn·a·by (bûr′nə-bē). City of SW B.C., Canada, near Vancouver. Pop. 131,599.

Bur·sa (bŏŏr-sä′, bûr′sə). City of NW Turkey, near the Sea of Marmara. Pop. 466,178.

Bu·run·di (bŏŏ-rōōn′dē). Country of E central Africa. Cap. Bujumbura. Pop. 3,864,000.

Byd·goszcz (bĭd′gŏshch). Industrial city of N Poland. Pop. 343,800.

Byz·an·tine Empire (bĭz′ən-tēn′, -tīn′). E part of the later Roman Empire.

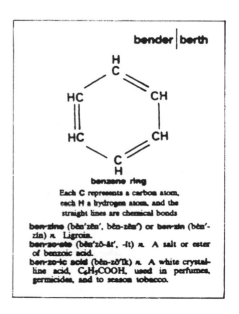

bender | berth

benzene ring

Each C represents a carbon atom, each H a hydrogen atom, and the straight lines are chemical bonds

ben·zine (bĕn′zēn′, bĕn-zēn′) or **ben·zin** (bĕn′-zĭn) *n.* Ligroin.

ben·zo·ate (bĕn′zō-āt′, -ĭt) *n.* A salt or ester of benzoic acid.

ben·zo·ic acid (bĕn-zō′ĭk) *n.* A white crystalline acid, C_6H_5COOH, used in perfumes, germicides, and to season tobacco.

Activity 4–9
Homographs

The words in bold letters in the sentences below are homographs. On a separate sheet of paper, number from one to eleven. Beside each number write the letter of the dictionary entry that correctly identifies the homograph as it is used in the sentence. The first has been done as an example.

A. bark—the sound a dog makes

B. bark—the outer covering of a tree

C. bark—a sailing ship with three to five masts

   1. Early settlers in America arrived in a **bark**.   **Answer:** C

   2. The **bark** was stripped from the aspen by a deer.

A. buffer—an implement used to shine or polish

B. buffer—something that lessens or absorbs the shock of impact

   3. The wall acted as a **buffer** and protected her from the oncoming car.

A. bunting—a light cloth used for making flags

B. bunting—a bird with a short, cone-shaped bill

C. bunting—a hooded sleeping bag for infants

   4. The baby was wrapped in a **bunting**.

   5. Betsy Ross may have used **bunting** in her first sewing project.

A. case—a specified instance

B. case—a container or receptacle

   6. The detective solved the **case** after discovering one more clue.

A. pit—a relatively deep hole in the ground

B. pit—the single, hard-shelled seed of certain fruits

   7. Unfamiliar with the land, he fell into the **pit**.

A. prop—a support or stay

B. prop—a stage property

C. prop—a propeller

   8. She used the crutch as a **prop**.

   9. The director said the **prop** for Scene Two was inappropriate.

A. **pry**—to look closely; to snoop

B. **pry**—to raise, move, or force open with a lever

10. He angrily accused his neighbor of trying to **pry**.

A. **rent**—periodic payment in return for the right to use the property of another

B. **rent**—an opening made by a rip

11. The gale-force winds left a gaping **rent** in the curtain.

Activity 4–10
Unit Review

In Unit 4, you have practiced using dictionary entries to find information about words and about people and places, as well. You might have been surprised to learn just how much information your dictionary contains. Using what you now know and the dictionary entries provided, answer the following questions. On a separate sheet of paper, number from one to fifteen, and begin.

1. Define *main entry*.
2. Define *syllabication*.
3. Syllabicate the word *dependent*.
4. Define *variant spellings*.
5. Give the variant spelling of the word *dependent*.
6. Define *etymology*.
7. Give the etymology of the word *deplete*.
8. What is the etymological meaning of the word *deplete?*
9. Define *inflected form*.
10. Give the inflected form of the word *deplane*.
11. Define *guide words*.
12. List the guide words for this dictionary entry page.
13. Define *homograph*.
14. List three parts of speech.
15. List all the parts of speech for the word *dependent*.

Exploring the Library/Media Center

EXPLORE (ĕk-splōr′) v. To investigate systematically

LIBRARY (lī′brĕr-ē) n. a repository for literary and artistic materials kept for reading or reference

MEDIA (mē′dē-ă) n. the agency by which something is conveyed or transferred

CENTER (sĕn′tər) n. a place of concentrated activity or influence

hat is it that you want to know? Maybe you have a term paper assignment and you need material on the life of Ernest Hemingway. Perhaps you are interested in collared lizards and don't know where to begin looking for information about them. To settle a bet you made with a friend, you may need to know how many home runs Dave Winfield hit in the 1983 World Series. No matter what kind of information you seek, the library/media center is the place to begin looking.

Library/media centers are designed with your needs as a student in mind. Why, then, is the card catalog a mystery? Why is searching a periodical index such an ordeal? And why is reading on microfilm a back issue of the newspaper so confusing? If the thought of having to go to your local library to do any of these makes you want to run for the door, relax and get comfortable, instead. This unit is designed to quickly and painlessly acquaint you with library services and materials.

Though libraries vary in arrangements, each has a collection that includes books, periodicals, microforms, and pamphlet materials. Some collections also include records, tapes, and videos, as well. The card catalog and other periodical indexes contain information to help you locate the various materials.

Your librarian can also help. Librarians and their assistants are there to make sure that the information you need is available to you. Of course, if you don't ask them questions, librarians can't know your needs. Don't be shy! There is no such thing as a dumb question.

A librarian can help you find information and also suggest sources you might not have considered.

Activity 5–1
Classification of Fiction

In most school and public libraries, books are classified and arranged on the shelves under the categories of fiction or nonfiction. Activity 5–1 deals with fiction books; Activity 5–2 discusses nonfiction books.

Writing that is based on imagination—that is not true—is called *fiction*. Fiction includes novels and short stories. In a library, fiction books are arranged alphabetically by the author's last name. For example, a book by James Michener will be found under the letter *M*. Collections of short stories written by several authors are arranged alphabetically by the collection editor's name.

Number a separate sheet of paper from one to five and arrange the following fiction books in the order they would appear on the library shelves.

1. *Siege of Silence* by A. J. Quinell

2. *The Land That Time Forgot* by E. R. Burroughs

3. *Follow the River* by J. A. Thom

4. *The Monkey Wrench Gang* by E. Abbey

5. *The Warrior's Path* by L. L'Amour

Activity 5-2
Classification of Nonfiction

A second major category of books on the shelves in library/media centers is the nonfiction category.

All books that are not novels or short stories—that are factual—are labeled *nonfiction*. Nonfiction materials are organized by two main classification systems: the Dewey decimal system, which uses numbers for identifying ten major subject categories, and the Library of Congress system, which uses letters for identifying twenty-one major categories. (See examples below.)

It is not important that you memorize either classification system. Just be aware that both systems are used, and that the LOC (Library of Congress) system is usually used in larger city and university libraries.

ABBREVIATED DEWEY DECIMAL CLASSIFICATION SCHEME

000–099	General Works
100–199	Philosophy and Psychology
200–299	Religion
300–399	Social Sciences
400–499	Language
500–599	Pure Sciences
600–699	Technology
700–799	The Arts
800–899	Literature
900–999	History

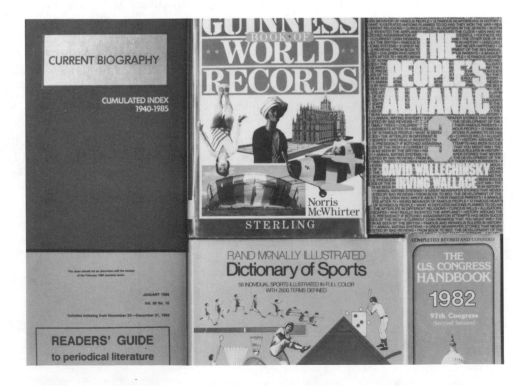

ABBREVIATED LIBRARY OF CONGRESS CLASSIFICATION SCHEME

A . . . . .General Works
B . . . . .Philosophy, Psychology, Religion
C . . . . .History: Auxiliary Sciences (Archaeology, Numismatics, Geneal-
　　　　　　　　　ogy, etc.)
D . . . . .History: General and Old World
E . . . . .History: American and U.S., general
F . . . . .History: American and U.S., local
G . . . . .Geography, Anthropology, Folklore, Dance, Sports
H . . . . .Social Sciences: Sociology, Business, and Economics
J . . . . .Political Science
K . . . . .Law
L . . . . .Education
M . . . . .Music
N . . . . .Fine Arts: Art and Architecture
P . . . . .Literature
Q . . . . .Science
R . . . . .Medicine
S . . . . .Agriculture
T . . . . .Technology
U . . . . .Military Science
V . . . . .Naval Science
Z . . . . .Bibliography and Library Science

Continuing on a separate sheet of paper, number from one to five again. List the identifying codes for the major categories in which books on the following topics would be found. Look at the classification schemes for the Dewey decimal system to help you decide.

1. Buddhism

2. Civil War (U.S.)

3. Mental disorders

4. Conversational Dutch

5. Modern music

Activity 5–3
Reading Call Numbers

In all libraries, nonfiction books are arranged on the shelves, or stacks, by their call numbers. Each book has its own call number made up of its classification code (either Dewey decimal or Library of Congress), as well as its own letter-number combinations, which indicates the book's author.

Dewey decimal call numbers should be read one line at a time. *Example:*

Complete call number 527.6 . . . . . .Line One (classification)
　　　　　　　　　　　J53 . . . . .Line Two (author)

The books are first arranged numerically, according to the numbers in Line One.
Example:

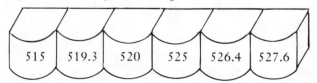

Line One　　515　519.3　520　525　526.4　527.6

The arrangement of Line Two is first alphabetical and then numerical, with the number in Line Two being read as a decimal number. Read J.3 followed by J.34 followed by J.4. **Example:**

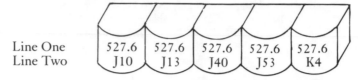

Line One
Line Two

| 527.6 | 527.6 | 527.6 | 527.6 | 527.6 |
| J10 | J13 | J40 | J53 | K4 |

The following numbers are call numbers of books classified under the Dewey decimal system. Arrange them in the correct order by call number, as if they were actual books. Then, using the ten main divisions of the Dewey decimal system, name the category to which each book would belong.

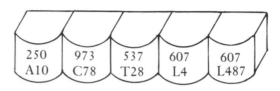

| 250 | 973 | 537 | 607 | 607 |
| A10 | C78 | T28 | L4 | L487 |

Activity 5–4
Determining Classification Groups Using Titles

The following titles clearly reveal their subject matter. List the authors and titles on the separate sheet of paper you are using. Opposite each, write the Dewey decimal classification group to which it belongs.

1. John Carroll, *The Study of Language*

2. J. Newton Friend, *Man and the Chemical Element*

3. Harry Emerson Fosdick, *The Man from Nazareth*

4. John Gunther, *Inside Latin America*

5. Ivor Brown, *Shakespeare in His Time*

Activity 5–5
Determining Classification Groups Using Dewey Numbers

The titles in the following list do not clearly indicate the subjects of the books. Determine the subject matter of each book by comparing the Dewey classification number after each title with the Dewey classification list. Number from one to five on a separate sheet of paper and write the letter of the correct answer beside the appropriate number.

1. *I Can Jump Puddles* (616)

   A. a novel

   B. a biography

   C. a book telling how a polio victim overcame hardships

2. *The Wild Duck* (808.8)

    A. a scientific book for biology class

    B. a book on hunting wild game

    C. a play

3. *The Crack in the Picture Window* (711)

    A. the history of glass

    B. an inquiry into the architecture of American housing developments

    C. a history of government foreclosures of mortgages

4. *Journey Into Light* (617.7)

    A. a biography

    B. the story of medical help for the blind

    C. a travel book

5. *Horsefeathers* (422)

    A. a book dealing with word origins

    B. a book of party games

    C. a book of veterinary medicine

Activity 5-6
Understanding the Card Catalog

The easiest way to find the books you want in the library is by using the card catalog. The card catalog contains alphabetically arranged cards listing the call numbers of each book in the library's collection. There are usually three cards for each book: an author card, a title card, and a subject card. You may also find a cross-reference card, referring you to another related topic listed in the card catalog.

The catalog cards also list information such as the book's publisher, the publication date, the number of pages, and whether the book includes illustrations.

Subject Card

> OWLS
>
> 598.97 Austing, G. Ronald
>
>   The World of the Great Horned Owl: Text and
>
> photographs by G. Ronald Austing and John B.
>
> Holt, Jr. New York: Lippincott, c 1968.
>
> 158 pp. illus. (Living World Books)

Title Card

The World of the Great Horned Owl.
598.97   Text and photographs by G. Ronald Austing and
John B. Holt, Jr. New York: Lippincott, c. 1968.
158 pp. illus. (Living World Books)

Author Card

Austing, G. Ronald
598.97   The World of the Great Horned Owl: Text and
photographs by G. Ronald Austing and John B.
Holt, Jr. New York: Lippincott, c 1968.
158 pp. illus. (Living World Books)
1. Owls 2. Birds, predator

Cross-reference Card

OWLS
see also
Birds, predator

Refer to the previous examples of cards from the card catalog for the book on owls. Number a separate sheet of paper from one to ten and try to answer the following questions:

1. What three ways are books usually listed in the card catalog?

2. What is the title of the book?

3. Who wrote the book?

4. Who is the publisher?

5. When was the book published?

6. What kind of a book does the Dewey decimal call number indicate it is?

7. Who was the photographer for this book?

8. How many pages does this book have?

9. What series is this book a part of?

10. What is another cross-reference other than the one given that might apply to owls?

The reference section contains a wealth of information.

Activity 5-7
Using the Card Catalog

Number a separate sheet of paper from one to five. Using the card catalog in your library/media center, find the author, title, and call number for each of the following:

1. A book written *by* Samuel Clemens (Mark Twain)

2. A book written *about* Samuel Clemens

3. A nonfiction book written about Africa

4. A collection of American poetry

5. A book about space travel

Activity 5-8
Using Reference Materials

Reference books are valuable information sources usually kept together in the reference section of the library. They must be used in the library; they cannot be checked out.

Before attempting to use any reference book for the first time, skim its introductory pages to learn how to use it and how to decode the symbols and other abbreviations used in that particular volume. Reference books include:

Dictionaries

In addition to the familiar collection of words and definitions, there are dictionaries on languages, medicine, math, and music, to name only a few.

Encyclopedias

Encyclopedias are one of the best places to begin looking for research materials. Here you will find articles on a variety of subjects written by experts. Topics are arranged alphabetically; the letters on the spine of each volume indicate the portion of the alphabet that volume covers.

Almanacs and Yearbooks

These volumes, published annually, summarize the previous year's events. They contain factual and statistical information on current developments in such areas as government, sports, economics, careers, and so on.

Biographical Reference Books

These books offer brief biographical sketches of notable people in all fields, worldwide. Some list living, currently prominent persons, while others refer to specific groups, such as actors or presidents.

Literary Reference Books and Books About Authors

Anything you need to know concerning literature can be found under this category. Find who wrote it or said it or where it came from by consulting such volumes as *Twentieth Century Authors, Bartlett's Familiar Quotations, Granger's Index to Poetry,* and *The Oxford Companion to American Literature.*

Periodicals

When doing research, you'll often find newspapers, magazines, and digests quite useful. They may be used to supplement information you find in books, or, for certain topics, they may be the only information source available. Some libraries keep back issues of periodicals on microforms (microfilm and microfiche) for convenient storage. Current events digests such as *Facts on File, A Matter of Fact,* and *Social Issues Resources Series, Inc. (SIRS)* are available in some libraries.

Maps and Atlases

Most libraries have a selection of atlases containing a variety of interesting data and maps. Where do Kudus roam when they are not in a zoo? Check the *Atlas of World Wildlife*. What is the highest mountain peak on each continent? Look in the *Rand McNally World Atlas*.

Vertical File

Usually found in filing cabinets accessible to library users, the vertical file contains the "et cetera" category in most libraries. This is the place you will find small pamphlets, booklets, catalogs, and clippings on a variety of topics. Depending on the rules at your library, information from the vertical file may sometimes be checked out.

Because you'll use them often, it's important to know where in your library the reference area is and what particular reference volumes are available there. To help you find out, take a trip to the reference area of your library and, on a separate sheet of paper, write the answers to the following questions. Be sure to note both the titles and page numbers of the reference books you use, as well as the answer to each question.

1. What is the height of the Statue of Liberty?

2. When is Richard Burton's birthday?

3. What is the difference in elevation between the highest and lowest points in the United States?

4. What is the language spoken in Jordan?

5. From what language do we get the word *recipe*?

6. Who is the author and what is the title of a poem in which these lines appear:

   > "And what is so rare as a day in June?
   > Then, if ever, came perfect days . . . ."

7. List the title of a catalog found in the vertical file.

8. What type of sporting events are featured in the latest issue of a newspaper kept in your library?

9. List the titles of two magazines that include information on health and nutrition.

10. What was the year women were first allowed to vote for the president of the United States? Who was elected that year?

Activity 5–9
Periodical Indexes

When you need to locate articles on a specific subject, you can sit down and browse through piles of magazines and stacks of newspapers. Or, you can save time and consult a periodical index. Periodical indexes enable you to find material on a given topic or by a specific author quickly.

At your local library, you may have access to the *Readers' Guide to Periodical Literature* in bound volumes, or you may be able to use an Infotrac system consisting of a computer and a compact disk. Either way, if you could compare the two you would find that they use basically the same form of entry.

An entry in the *Readers' Guide* or on Infotrac is called a *citation*. Once you understand the format, you can read the citations easily. A citation looks something like this:

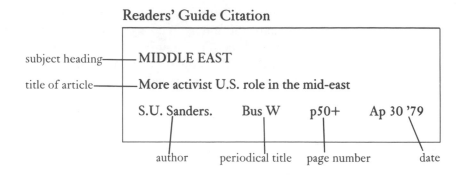

Readers' Guide Citation

subject heading——**MIDDLE EAST**

title of article——**More activist U.S. role in the mid-east**

S.U. Sanders.   Bus W   p50+   Ap 30 '79

author   periodical title   page number   date

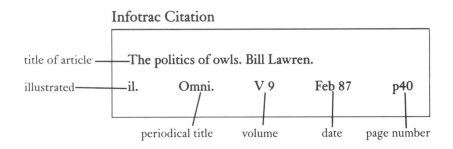

Infotrac Citation

title of article ——The politics of owls. Bill Lawren.

illustrated——il.   Omni.   V 9   Feb 87   p40

periodical title   volume   date   page number

Periodical indexes help you find materials on a specific topic quickly.

Notice that each citation includes abbreviations. Some, like the examples given, are very easy to decipher. Others, however, are more difficult, so always check the list of abbreviations given at the beginning of the index for a complete translation.

As you do research, get in the habit of writing down the entire citation, along with the title of the index in which you found it. This will simplify your task when you have to list the sources of your information.

As you can imagine, storage is becoming an ever-increasing problem in this age of mass communication. Many libraries use microforms to solve storage problems. The term *microform* describes information that has been photographed and reduced in size. Libraries often store newspapers and magazines on microfiche or microfilm—two types of microforms frequently used. Special machines called *readers,* some equipped with printers, are required in order for you to use the microforms. Ask your librarian to help you learn to use the reader machine.

The names of the publications found in the microform collection are sometimes listed in the card catalog. Other libraries list microforms in a special catalog. No matter where you find the cards in your library, they will look something like this:

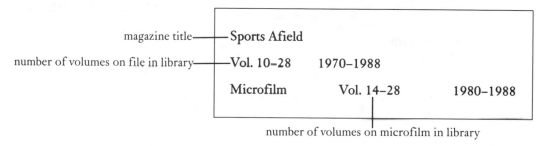

Now that you are more familiar with periodical indexes, number a separate sheet of paper from one to ten and list two complete citations for each of the following topics. Use the *Readers' Guide to Periodical Literature* or Infotrac to find the magazine articles.

A. TV advertising

B. environmental control

C. photography

D. baseball

E. elections

Activity 5–10
Using the *Readers' Guide to Periodical Literature*

Using the sample pages from the *Readers' Guide,* list the names of the magazines that include articles on the following topics. If there is more than one article for the topic, list only the first magazine.

A. sports cars—design

B. sports medicine

C. stage fright

D. stars—age

E. stars—new

F. List the complete citation for an article on Bruce Springsteen that includes illustrations.

SPORTS CARS—Design—*cont.*
New Ferrari seen—despite denials. il *Motor Trend* 40:24 My '88

History
Carrera RS 2.7 [Porsche] J. Rusz. il *Road & Track* 39:55 My '88
Learning the hard way [TVR] P. Bingham. il *Motor Trend* 40:118-19 My '88

Testing
Chevrolet Corvette [cover story] C. Csere. il *Car and Driver* 33:44-8+ My '88
Porsche 911 Club Sport [cover story] il *Road & Track* 39:50-4 My '88
Porsche 944 Turbo S. J. Karr. il *Motor Trend* 40:72-3+ My '88
The Schwarzenegger of muscle cars [Corvette] W. J. Hampton. il *Business Week* p161 My 9 '88
SPORTS CARS, RACING *See* Automobiles, Racing
SPORTS CLUBS
See also
Achilles Track Club
Atoms Track Club
How to be a social smash: smart sets [tennis clubs; special section] il *Harper's Bazaar* 121:142-5+ My '88
SPORTS FANS
See also
Baseball fans
Boxing fans
SPORTS JOURNALISM
Hoops but no scoops [press coverage restricted at U.S. Olympic basketball trials] A. Wolff. il *Sports Illustrated* 68:34-6 My 30 '88
Seduced and abandoned [poor press coverage of stock car racing] A. Girdler. il *Road & Track* 39:28 My '88
SPORTS MANAGEMENT *See* Sports—Organization and administration
SPORTS MEDICINE
See also
Running—Accidents and injuries
Tennis—Accidents and injuries
Pain, pain, go away. D. Groves. il *Women's Sports & Fitness* 10:32-4 Ap '88
SPORTS OFFICIATING
See also
Baseball, Professional—Umpiring
Hockey, Professional—Refereeing
Tennis—Tournaments—Officiating
SPORTS RECORDS
See also
Boat speed records
Fishing records
SPORTS SHOES *See* Footwear
SPORTS WRITING *See* Sports journalism
SPORTSCASTERS *See* Cable television—Sports; Radio broadcasting—Sports; Television broadcasting—Sports
SPORTSMEN *See* Athletes
SPORTSMIND (FIRM)
Breaking through. J. Harris. il *Esquire* 109:154-7 My '88
SPORTSWOMEN *See* Women athletes
SPORTSWRITING *See* Sports journalism
SPRADLING, RICHARD
(jt. auth) *See* Buford, Constance W., and Spradling, Richard
SPRAYING AND DUSTING
See also
Pesticides
SPREADS (FOOD)
Camembert spread with walnut flat bread. il *Better Homes and Gardens* 66:118+ Ap '88
Haroseth: versatile sweet fruit spread [Passover tradition] il *Better Homes and Gardens* 66:143+ Ap '88
SPREADSHEETS (COMPUTER PROGRAMS)
Testing
Moving to a new dimension [Boeing Calc] M. Bryan. il *Personal Computing* 12:220 Ap '88
SPRING
See also
May
SPRING CLEANING *See* House cleaning
SPRING DINNERS *See* Dinners and dining
SPRINGER, NANCY
Sparrow's fall [story] il *U.S. Catholic* 53:32-7 Ap '88
SPRINGFIELD (MASS.)
Economic conditions
The Springfield 'miracle'. J. Nocera. il *Newsweek* 111:45-6+ Je 6 '88

SPRINGSTEEN, BRUCE
Tangled up in Bob [address, January 20, 1988] *Harper's* 276:28-9+ Ap '88
about
Bruce Springsteen's Tunnel vision [cover story] S. Pond. il pors *Rolling Stone* p38-42 My 5 '88
SPRINT (WORD PROCESSOR PROGRAM) *See* Word processors and processing—Programming
SPRINTING *See* Track and field athletics
SPROCKETT, DOC
Battery power. *Flower and Garden* 32:91-2 Ap/My '88
SQL (STRUCTURED QUERY LANGUAGE) *See* Structured Query Language (Computer language)
SQUAB COOKING *See* Cooking—Poultry
SSC *See* Superconducting Super Collider
SSMC INC.
Can Paul Bilzerian fatten Singer for the kill? R. Mitchell. il por *Business Week* p43-4 My 16 '88
ST. ELSEWHERE [television program] *See* Television program reviews—Single works
ST. LOUIS (MO.) *See* Saint Louis (Mo.)
ST. PAUL'S CATHEDRAL CHOIR
Musical events:
Concert in St. Bartholomew's Church in New York. A. Porter. *The New Yorker* 64:98-9 My 16 '88
STABILITY OF AUTOMOBILES *See* Automobiles—Stability and stabilizers
STABLES, CONVERTED *See* Houses, Remodeled
STACHYS BYZANTINA *See* Lambs ears (Plant)
STADD, COURTNEY
about
Commercializing space: a conversation with Courtney Stadd. J. Muncy. por *Space World* Y-5-293:23-6 My '88
STADIUM ORGANISTS *See* Organists
STAGE *See* Theater
STAGE FRIGHT
Curing stage fright [musicians; research by Duncan Clark] *USA Today (Periodical)* 116:11 Ap '88
STAGE WEST THEATRE RESTAURANTS
An appetite for hits. P. Young. il *Maclean's* 101:50 My 23 '88
STAIRCASES *See* Stairways
STAIRWAYS
See also
Hand railings
Upgrade of unsafe stairway. D. Johnson. il *The Family Handyman* 38:82-3 My/Je '88
STALIN, JOSEPH, 1879-1953
about
A conversation with Stalin. V. V. Karpov. il *New Perspectives Quarterly* 5:51-3 Spr '88
STALKER, JOHN
Grave lies [excerpt from The Stalker affair] il *Life* 11:154+ My '88
STALLONE, JACQUELINE
about
Yo, mama! The wrestling Stallone, Sly's mother, Jackie, returns to the ring with a stable of Rambettes. S. K. Reed. il pors *People Weekly* 29:96-8 My 23 '88
STALLS, AIRPLANE *See* Airplanes, Business—Stalling
STAMINA *See* Endurance
STAMPS, POSTAGE *See* Postage stamps
STANDARD OIL CO. (OHIO)
See also
Standard Oil Company
STANDARD OIL COMPANY
Hearst's little time bomb [incriminating letters by J. D. Archbold of Standard Oil Company to various state and federal officials acquired by W. R. Hearst] P. Baida. il por *American Heritage* 39:18-19+ Ap '88
STANDS (MACHINE) *See* Machinery—Stands, tables, etc.
STANFORD UNIVERSITY
Excellence under the palm trees. T. A. Sancton. il *Time* 131:74-6 My 16 '88
Why the West? [defense of Western civilization] W. J. Bennett. il *National Review* 40:37-9 My 27 '88
STANFORD UNIVERSITY PRESS
Stanford to publish massive collection of London's letters. W. Goldstein. *Publishers Weekly* 233:36-7 Ap 29 '88
STAPHYLOCOCCAL DISEASES
See also
Toxic shock syndrome
STAR CHARTS *See* Astronomy—Charts, diagrams, etc.
STAR MAPS *See* Astronomy—Charts, diagrams, etc.
STAR WARS DEFENSE PROGRAM *See* Strategic Defense Initiative
STARCH
See also
Cornstarch

STARCK, PHILIPPE, 1950?-
about
Starck reality. L. Campbell. il *House & Garden* 160:38-40
Mr '88
STARGARDT'S DISEASE
Starring in track, tennis and soccer, Laurinda Mulhaupt
won't let blindness put her on the sidelines. K. Gross.
il pors *People Weekly* 29:119-21 My 23 '88
STARK, ELIZABETH
Beyond rivalry. il *Psychology Today* 22:61-3 Ap '88
STARR, DOUGLAS
Preserving pieces of the puzzle. il *National Wildlife* 26:4-13
Ap/My '88
STARR, JEROLD M., 1941-
A curriculum for teaching about the Vietnam War. *The
Education Digest* 53:28-31 Ap '88
STARS
See also
Astrology
Astronomy
Black holes (Astronomy)
Constellations
Galaxies
Age
How old is the Milky Way? *Sky and Telescope* 75:463-4
My '88
Charts, diagrams, etc.
See Astronomy—Charts, diagrams, etc.
Evolution
See also
Pulsars
Cosmic cloud without a heart [W49A star-forming region;
research by William John Welch and others] il *Discover*
9:10+ Ap '88
Journeys on the H-R diagram. J. B. Kaler. il *Sky and
Telescope* 75:482-5 My '88
Magnetic properties
Giant starspots on Lambda Andromedae [research by
James C. Kemp] *Sky and Telescope* 75:465-6 My '88
STARS, DOUBLE
New explanation for an old nova [Nova Cygni 1975;
research by Peter Stockman and others] D. E. Thomsen.
Science News 133:229 Ap 9 '88
STARS, NEW
New explanation for an old nova [Nova Cygni 1975;
research by Peter Stockman and others] D. E. Thomsen.
Science News 133:229 Ap 9 '88
STARS, VARIABLE
See also
Supernovas
Giant starspots on Lambda Andromedae [research by
James C. Kemp] *Sky and Telescope* 75:465-6 My '88
STARS AND BARS [film] *See* Motion picture
reviews—Single works
STARSHIP AIRPLANES *See* Airplanes, Business
START TALKS *See* Strategic Arms Reduction Talks
STARVATION
See also
Famines
STATE AND ART *See* Art and state
STATE AND CHURCH *See* Church and state
STATE AND EDUCATION *See* Education and state
STATE AND ENVIRONMENT *See* Environmental policy
STATE AND INDUSTRY *See* Industry and state
STATE AND LIBRARIES *See* Libraries and state
STATE AND LITERATURE *See* Literature and state
STATE AND MEDICINE *See* Medical policy
STATE AND SCIENCE *See* Science and state
STATE COURTS *See* Courts
STATE DEPT. (U.S.) *See* United States. Dept. of State
STATE EMPLOYEES
See also
AFSCME
STATE FINANCE
See also
Finance—Massachusetts
Big states, big gaps. T. Smart and H. Gleckman. il *Business
Week* p30-1 Je 6 '88
STATE SALES TAX *See* Sales tax
STATES, IDEAL *See* Utopias
STATES (U.S.)
States and Capitals [educational video games] E. Larsen
and M. D. Perry, Jr. il *Compute!* 10:80-2 Ap '88
STATHOPLOS, DEMMIE
One heavenly Star. il *Sports Illustrated* 68:32-3 My 30
'88
STATIC ELECTRICITY
How to map electrically charged patches with parsley,
sage, rosemary and thyme. J. Walker. il *Scientific
American* 258:114-17 Ap '88

STATMAN, MARK
(jt. auth) *See* Doyle, Kate, and Statman, Mark
STAUB, AUGUST W.
The mandate of the arts educator for cultural leadership:
somewhere between catering and contempt. *Design for
Arts in Education* 89:48-50 Mr/Ap '88
STAVOLE, NADINE
about
I showed my body who's boss! il pors *Mademoiselle*
94:60 Ap '88
STEAK COOKING *See* Cooking—Meat
STEALING
See also
Art thefts
Cattle—Theft
Credit card crimes
Embezzlement
STEALTH AIRPLANES *See* Airplanes, Military
STEAMSHIPS AND STEAMBOATS
See also
Ocean liners
STEARIC ACID
The good news about 'good fat' [stearic acid found to
lower cholesterol] il *U.S. News & World Report*
104:12-13 My 23 '88
Meaty matters [stearic acid found to lower cholesterol]
il *Time* 131:79 My 23 '88
STEEL, RONALD
Why a Democrat can't end the cold war. il *New
Perspectives Quarterly* 5:39-43 Spr '88
STEEL INDUSTRY
See also
McLouth Steel Products Corporation
United Steelworkers of America
STEEL SHOT *See* Shot
STEEL WORKERS
See also
United Steelworkers of America
STEELSMITH, RICK
about
Rick's got some tricks. J. Garrity. il pors *Sports Illustrated*
68:71-2+ My 9 '88
STEGER, WILL
North to the Pole [condensation]; ed. by Paul Schurke.
il *Reader's Digest* 132:229-34+ My '88
STEGMAIER, MARK E.
Gary Bowling. il *American Artist* 52:56-61+ My '88
STEHLIN, DORI
The silent epidemic of hip fractures. il *FDA Consumer*
22:18-23 My '88
STEIN, FRANCES PATIKY
about
Jet-set extras. il por *Harper's Bazaar* 121:40 My '88
STEIN, HARRY
Mates for life [excerpt from One of the guys] il *Glamour*
85:106+ Ap '88
STEIN, MARVIN, AND ABRAMS, MAXINE
How to stop making yourself sick. il *Good Housekeeping*
206:72+ Ap '88
STEIN, SUSAN R., 1949-
Thomas Jefferson's traveling desks. bibl f il *Antiques*
133:1156-9 My '88
STEINBACH, HAIM
about
Haim Steinbach: shelf life. H. Cotter. bibl f il *Art in
America* 76:156-63+ My '88
STEINBERG, LILLI
about
Refund sleuth Lilli Steinberg wrings money from phone
bills. il por *People Weekly* 29:95 My 23 '88
STEINGARTEN, JEFFREY
Fish without fire. il *House & Garden* 160:176-7+ Mr
'88
Takeout heaven? il *House & Garden* 160:156-7+ Ap '88
STEMPEL, ROBERT C.
about
GM faces reality [cover story] J. B. Treece. il pors *Business
Week* p114-18+ My 9 '88
STENSIÖ, ERIK ANDERSSON
about
A tale of three pictures. S. J. Gould. il *Natural History*
97:14+ My '88
STEPAN, ALFRED
The last days of Pinochet? il por *The New York Review
of Books* 35:32-5 Je 2 '88
STEPS *See* Stairways
STEREO LOUDSPEAKERS *See* Loudspeakers
STEREO SOUND SYSTEMS *See* Audio systems
STEREOCHEMISTRY
See also
Conformational analysis

Activity 5-11
Mini Research Project

Now you can practice your newly acquired library skills. We have carefully divided the project into manageable steps. You'll need to allow several hours to complete this project. You must have access to a library as you work. Follow these steps:

A. **Choose a topic that interests you.** You may know very little or a lot about this topic, but you should definitely choose a topic you want to know more about. Be specific rather than broad in your choice of topic.

B. **Do the research.**

1. Look up the topic in either the *Readers' Guide* or on Infotrac.

2. List three or four complete citations for your topic. If you limit yourself to one article, that periodical might not be available, and you will have to begin again.

3. Check the periodicals listed in your citations against the "Magazine Holdings Directory" (a list of magazines in your library) to be sure that your library has that particular periodical available. (No library has funds or room for all the periodicals published.)

4. For each citation, you will be asked to fill out a periodical request slip that looks something like this:

PERIODICAL REQUEST SLIP

Name of Magazine _____

Date of Issue: Month _____ Day ____ Year ____

Volume _____   Page _____

Your name _____

If the periodicals are not kept in open stacks, your librarian will get them for you.

5. *Save* the periodical request slips when you have the magazines or newspapers. You will need the slips to list your sources.

6. Read the articles carefully, taking notes on their contents.

C. **Write the summary.**

1. Write your name in the upper right-hand corner of a separate sheet of paper. Below that, list the name of this class and the date.

2. On the first line, in the center, write the title of your summary.

3. Using your notes, summarize what you have read. Make it interesting to your reader. Use your own words—not the author's.

4. On a separate sheet of paper entitled "Bibliography," list the complete citations for all of the articles you read to make your summary. Arrange the citations alphabetically according to magazine title.

5. Your instructor will want to see the periodical request slips you filled out, in addition to your summary and bibliography.

Activity 5–12
Unit Review

Number a separate sheet of paper from one to thirty. After reading the question and referring to the typed entry, select the correct multiple-choice answer or the appropriate answer to fill in the blank. Write your answer beside the corresponding number on your paper.

973.9

Lo

    Lord, Walter

       The good years; from 1900 to the first World War.

    Harper, 1960.

      369 p., illus., 32 plates, maps.

    1. U.S. - Civilization 2. U.S. History - 1898 3. Child Labor - U.S.

---

1. The card shown would be found in the card catalog filed under:

    A. Lo.   C. Wa.

    B. 973.9.   D. The.

2. The card shown is called a(n):

    A. title card.   C. subject card.

    B. author card.   D. all of the above

3. The author of the book is:

    A. Lord Walter.   C. Harper.

    B. Walter Lord.   D. none of the above

4. The title of the book is:

    A. Lord Walter.

    B. The good years; from 1900 to the first World War.

    C. The good years.

    D. none of the above

5. The subject of this book is:

    A. U.S.—Civilization.   C. Child Labor—U.S.

    B. U.S. History—1898.   D. all of the above

6. The call number of this book is:

    A. 973.9.   C. Lord.

    B. 973.9   D. none of the above
       Lo

7. The above book is:

    A. nonfiction.   C. reference.

    B. fiction.   D. none of the above

8. The book was published by _____.

9. It was published in _____.

10. The abbreviation *illus.* means _____.

790
Se

    DANCING

    Seaton, Don Cash

       Physical Education Handbook, 4th ed., Englewood

    Cliffs, N.J., Prentice-Hall, 1965. 3. Child Labor - U.S.

    365 p., illus.

11. The card shown is a(n):

    A. title card.   C. subject card.

    B. author card.   D. all of the above

12. If you were looking in the card catalog for the card shown, you would look in:

    A. the *Da* drawer.   C. the *Ph* drawer.

    B. the *Se* drawer.   D. all of the above

13. The author of this book is:

    A. Seaton Don Cash.   C. Seaton Cash Don.

    B. Don Cash Seaton.   D. Cash Don Seaton.

14. The title of the book is:

    A. Dancing.   C. Seaton, Don Cash.

    B. Physical Education   D. none of the above
       Handbook.

15. The call number of this book is:

    A. 790.   C. Seaton.

    B. 790   D. none of the above
      Se

16. The publisher is _____.

17. It was published in what year? _____.

18. *4th ed.* means _____.

SPACE Flight

           Manned flights

Charts may guide return from moon. H. Taylor.

Time   89:51   Je 25 '86

19. The title of the magazine article is:

    A. SPACE Flight.

    B. Manned flights.

    C. Charts may guide return from moon.

    D. none of the above

20. The subject of the article is:

    A. Manned flights.

    B. SPACE Flight.

    C. both of the above

    D. Charts may guide return from moon.

21. The author of the article is _____.

22. The name of the magazine is _____.

23. The volume number of the magazine is _____.

24. The page(s) the article is found on is (are) _____.

25. The date the magazine was published is _____.

> New way of living; excerpt from a new kind of
> country.   il   McCalls   105:193–200   My 19 '87

---

26. The title of the article is _____.

27. The article is taken from what larger work? _____

28. The article appears in what magazine? _____

29. Which volume? _____

30. What is the date of the magazine? _____

Answer Key

Answers are provided for most activities in this book. Answers are not provided for activities with open-ended questions or for activities that require personal responses.

UNIT ONE

Activity 1–1

1. *What You Need to Know About Developing Study Skills, Taking Notes & Tests, Using Dictionaries & Libraries*
2. Marcia J. Coman and Kathy L. Heavers
3. 1991
4. number of chapters: 5; number of pages: 96; title of the most interesting chapter: Answers will vary.
6. Pictures, charts, illustrations, and questions at the ends of chapters are included. There are no graphs or maps, nor do pages have a lot of white space.
7. Answers will vary.
8. Answer Key

Activity 1–2

A. Look at the title, author, and publication (or copyright) date.
B. Read the preface or introduction.
C. Look at the table of contents, reading chapter titles, main headings, and subheadings and turning them into questions.
D. Flip through the book, looking at any charts, pictures, captions, and graphs.
E. Evaluate the difficulty of the material.
F. Know your purpose for reading the book.
G. Turn to the back of the book to see what study aids are included.
1. Previewing your text is looking at the book before a class begins to determine what it contains.
2. The value of previewing your text is that you will have a better idea of the following:
    A. what will be covered in the book and in the class;
    B. how difficult the material will be for you;
    C. the format of the book;
    D. the location of the study aids, graphs, charts, pictures, and so on.
       You will be more informed and prepared, save time, and perhaps earn better grades.

Activity 1–3

Answers will vary according to individual study environments; you may list problems such as being interrupted by telephone calls, siblings, or parents, having no room of your own in which to study, having no desk, and so on.

Activity 1–4

1. Study in the same place every day.
2. Study in a quiet place.
3. Learn to block out lower levels of noise.
4. Create a study center.
5. Collect all materials before beginning.
6. Face a blank wall.
7. Eliminate distractions.
8. Use proper lighting.
9. Have proper ventilation.
10. Have a working surface that is large enough.
11. Clear away the clutter.
12. Prop book at 30-degree angle when reading.
13. Have one subject at a time on the desk.
14. Complete one task before beginning another.

Activity 1–5

Solutions will vary depending on the problems listed in Activity 1–3.

Activity 1–7

1. Make a plan.
2. Make a written list of what you need to accomplish and the amount of time each task will take.
3. Study at the time of day you can concentrate best.
4. Determine your study sequence (hardest assignments to easiest, alternate activities, first things first according to importance).
5. Take breaks from studying.
6. A time frame is optional.
7. Be flexible.
8. Sequence your tasks.

Activity 1–11

SQ3R Method of Study
S = Survey
1. Look at the title.
2. Read the first paragraph or introduction.
3. Read the first sentence of each of the other paragraphs.
4. Read the last paragraph or conclusion.

Q = Question
Formulate your own list of questions using the following:
1. questions listed at the end of the chapter;
2. questions provided by the instructor;
3. headings that can be turned into questions;
4. questions on worksheets, quizzes, or tests.

R = Read
Read the material to answer the questions you have listed.

R = Recite
Recite aloud or to yourself the answers to the questions.

R = Review
After time has elapsed, review the answers to your questions.

Activity 1–13

UNIT REVIEW

I. Multiple Choice
1. D. Any of the above
2. D. All of the above
3. B. Ten minutes
4. C. They are absolutely essential, or your concentration will falter.
5. B. Flexible

II. Listing
6 to 12. A. See answers for Activity 1–4.
        B. See answers for Activity 1–2, Question 1.
13 to 17. S = Survey; Q = Question; R = Read; R = Recite; R = Review

III. Short Essay
18. A. See answers for Activity 1–2, Questions 2 and 3.
    B. Concentration will improve; grades will improve; time will be saved. Answers will vary regarding changes made and resulting benefits.
    C. Answers will vary.

UNIT TWO

Activity 2–1

I. Need to develop good NT skills
   A. Concentrate on lecture
   B. Pick out imp. pts./exclude unimp. pts.
   C. Develop system
   D. Streamline NT so imp. pts. not omitted
   E. Review notes

Activity 2–3

1. Main idea: "One of the most important skills for you to develop early in your school career is that of taking notes in an organized manner."
2. first sentence
3. Main idea: "One of the first steps toward developing an organized note-taking system is being able to recognize the author's main idea."
4. first sentence
5. I. Main idea or topic sentence found in number of positions
6. A. First sentence
   B. Last sentence
   C. First and last sentences
   D. Between first and last sentences
   E. Split—part in one sentence and part in another
   F. Not stated at all
7. I. Most widely used method: the Outline
     A. Format is specific structure
     B. It's concise
     C. Notes well organized
     D. Notes easily remembered

Activity 2–4

Paragraph One
I. Three reasons for good notes
   A. Helps pay attention
   B. Helps remember
   C. Helps organize ideas

Paragraph Two
I. Steps to keep mind from wandering
   A. Choose seat carefully
   B. Avoid friends
   C. Avoid personal matters
   D. Stay awake and alert

Activity 2–5

Full Signals, Paragraph One: *First; Second; Third*
Full Signals, Paragraph Two: *First*
Half Signals, Paragraph Two: *Next; In addition; Last*

Activity 2–10

1. Leave periods off abbreviations.
   ex for *example*   no for *number*
   st for *street*   dif for *different*

2. Use common symbols.
   & for *and*   + for *plus* or *positive*
   × for *times (multiplication)*   # for *number*

3. Eliminate vowels.
   If you are unfamiliar with conventional shorthand, the no-vowel system may save you when you have an instructor who has a very rapid speaking style. Try to read the following set of notes taken using the no-vowel technique:

   Ths prgrph ws wrttn n th "n vwl" nd th "bbrvtd" tchnq. Nt ll stdnts lk 2 tk nts ths wy, bt t wrks wll 4 sm. f y cn rd ths, y ndrstnd th mssg.

4. Use word beginnings.
   intro for *introduction*   com for *committee*
   info for *information*   rep for *representative*

5. Add "s" to abbreviations to form plurals.
   exs for *examples*   abbs for *abbreviations*
   mos for *months*   yrs for *years*

6. Use personal shorthand.
   Make up abbreviations that are meaningful to you. They need not make sense to other people; if you understand them and they save you time, they are valuable. Did you, for example, use *NT* anywhere in this unit instead of *note taking*?

   w/ for *with*   4 for *four* or *for*
   w/o for *without*   B4 for *before*

Activity 2–11

UNIT REVIEW

I. True–False

1. True	3. False	5. True	7. True	9. False
2. True	4. False	6. False	8. False	10. True

II. Five Methods of Note Taking

Outline	Listing		
I.	Heading	**Patterning:**	any drawing, pattern, or diagram
A.	1.		
1.	2.	**Margin Notes:**	one to three key words written in the margin identifying main ideas
a.	3.		
etc.	4.		
	5.		
	etc.	**Highlighting:**	using a highlighter to mark main points in a textbook, set of notes, etc.

III. Listing

16. Leave periods off abbreviations
17 to 18. (examples)
19. Eliminate vowels
20 to 21. (examples)
22. Use word beginnings

22 to 24. (examples)
25. Add "s" to abbreviations to form plurals
26 to 27. (examples)
28. Use personal shorthand
29 to 30. (examples)

IV. Short Essay.

31. Answers will vary.
32. Answers will vary.

UNIT THREE

Activity 3–1

Layer One: no repetition—short-term, unreliable memory.
Layer Two: some repetition—slightly longer retention, but not reliable.
Layer Three: repetition and writing down the information—fairly good retention.
Layer Four: repeating and writing down information over a period of three to six days—excellent retention.

Activity 3–2

Answers will vary but should include some of the suggestions listed for Activity 3–3.

Activity 3–5

Answers will vary but should resemble the list of strategies in Activity 3–5.

Activity 3–6

Answers will vary but should include most of the items found in Activity 3–6.

Activity 3–7

Term	Answer Would Include:
A. List	a numbered list of words, sentences, or comments
B. Outline	a series of main ideas supported by secondary ideas, etc.
C. Define	meanings but no details; this is often a matter of giving a memorized definition
D. Criticize	your own judgment or opinion based on reasons; good and bad points should be included
E. Summarize	a brief, condensed account of the main ideas; omit details
F. Trace	details, progress, or history of the topic from beginning to end
G. Describe	details or a verbal picture of the topic
H. Diagram	a chart, graph, or geometric drawing with labels and a brief explanation, if needed
I. Compare	both the similarities and the differences
J. Contrast	the differences only
K. Discuss	reasons pro and con with details
L. Justify	prove or give reasons

Activity 3–8

Answers should address the following topics:
- What kind of questions did my instructor include?
- What material did my instructor cover—textbook? lecture notes? exercises from class?
- What was my instructor looking for in my answers?
- What were my strengths in answering the questions?
- What were my weak areas?
- What test-taking strategies do I need to use again next time?
- What changes do I need to make?

Activity 3–9

UNIT REVIEW

I. True–False

1. False	5. False	9. False	13. True	17. True
2. True	6. False	10. False	14. True	18. True
3. True	7. True	11. False	15. False	19. False
4. True	8. True	12. False	16. False	20. True

II. Matching

21. H. contrast	25. A. list	28. G. compare
22. C. define	26. F. describe	29. B. outline
23. E. trace	27. I. discuss	30. D. criticize
24. J. justify		

III. Listing

31 to 37. Answers will vary but should include information from Activity 3–3.

IV. Essay

38. A. Answers should come from Activity 3–4.

B. Answers should come from Activity 3–5.

C. Answers for this essay question should include:

Layer One: no repetition—short-term, unreliable memory.

Layer Two: some repetition—slightly longer retention, but not reliable.

Layer Three: repetition and writing down the information—fairly good retention.

Layer Four: repeating and writing down information over a period of three to six days—excellent retention.

UNIT FOUR

Activity 4-1

Section One

1. <u>v</u>   w   <u>x</u>
2. <u>a</u>   b   <u>c</u>
3. <u>w</u>   x   <u>y</u>
4. <u>l</u>   m   <u>n</u>
5. <u>i</u>   j   <u>k</u>
6. <u>r</u>   s   <u>t</u>
7. <u>f</u>   g   <u>h</u>
8. <u>b</u>   c   <u>d</u>
9. <u>k</u>   l   <u>m</u>
10. <u>p</u>   q   <u>r</u>

Section Two

1. b   <u>c</u>   d
2. v   <u>w</u>   x
3. j   <u>k</u>   l
4. q   <u>r</u>   s
5. a   <u>b</u>   c
6. i   <u>j</u>   k
7. w   <u>x</u>   y
8. e   <u>f</u>   g
9. t   <u>u</u>   v
10. m   <u>n</u>   o
11. f   <u>g</u>   h
12. g   <u>h</u>   i

Section Three

1. b   f   g   (a)
2. m   p   z   (l)
3. r   x   (c)   g
4. (q)   s   v   y
5. w   t   (m)   p
6. l   (f)   s   k
7. t   s   (r)   x
8. l   p   (d)   q
9. h   (e)   k   i
10. (i)   m   k   q

Activity 4-2

1. easement, east, easy
2. garage, garbage, grand
3. location, locomotion, locomotive
4. sheet, shelter, shield
5. clang, clangor, clank
6. twilight, twinkle, twist
7. waste, wonder, wood
8. incident, indent, indicator
9. atomic, atrocious, attach
10. upstage, upstairs, upstart

Activity 4-4

1. guide words
2. main entry
3. syllabication
4. diacritical marks
5. part of speech
6. variant
7. inflected forms
8. etymology
9. pronunciation key

Activity 4–5

1. Mexican Spanish;
   no etymological meaning
2. Greek; market
3. Old French; to enclose
4. Old French; to seize
5. Portuguese; a flightless
   bird of South America
6. Latin; to include
7. French; again
8. Anglo-Norman; to coat
   or decorate with enamel
9. Old English; no
   etymological meaning
10. Old French; to block up
11. to 17. empress, enamor,
        enclave, encounter, encourage,
        encroach, encumber

Activity 4–6

Section One: Syllabication
1. gla•cial
2. glad•i•a•tor
3. glam•our
4. glad•i•o•lus
5. gla•ci•ate

Section Two: Inflected Forms
6. gave, given, giving
7. glaciated, glaciating
8. glamorized, glamorizing
9. gladder, gladdest
10. girded or girt, girding

Activity 4–7

Section One
1. glacier—J
2. authentic—G
3. author—C
4. enact—A
5. enclose—E
6. brunette—B
7. brow—F
8. encourage—D
9. gist—H
10. August—I

Section Two
During a football game, one of the players had a couple of fingers badly smashed. The team doctor examined and dressed the hand.

"Doctor," asked the player anxiously, "will I be able to play the piano?" "Certainly you will," promised the doctor.

"You're wonderful, Doctor," said the happy player. "I could never play the piano before!"

Activity 4–8

1. the fifteenth U.S. President
2. Brasilia
3.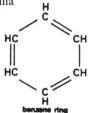

benzene ring

4. ••
5. also known as
6. as soon as possible
7. C_6H_5COOH
8. William Frederick Cody
9. Hill in Charleston, Mass.,
   near site of first major
   Revolutionary War battle in 1775
10. 1924

Activity 4–9

1. C
2. B
3. B
4. C
5. A
6. A
7. A
8. A
9. B
10. A
11. B

Activity 4–10

UNIT REVIEW

1. the word you are looking up; printed in bold type
2. the word divided into syllables by centered dots
3. de•pend•ent
4. two or more correct spellings of the same word

    5. dependant
    6. the origin of the word
    7. Latin
    8. to empty
    9. spelling changes in the word due to plurals or tense changes
  10. deplaned, deplaning
  11. the words at the top of the dictionary page representing the first and last word entries on the page
  12. denizen, deplore
  13. words with the same spelling and pronunciation but with different meanings
  14. Answers may include any three of the following: noun, pronoun, verb, adverb, adjective, interjection, preposition, or conjunction.
  15. adjective, noun

UNIT FIVE

Activity 5–1

1. *The Monkey Wrench Gang* by E. Abbey
2. *The Land That Time Forgot* by E. R. Burroughs
3. *The Warrior's Path* by L. Lamour
4. *Siege of Silence* by A. J. Quinell
5. *Follow the River* by J. A. Thom

Activity 5–2

1. 200–299
2. 900–999
3. 100–199
4. 400–499
5. 700–799

Activity 5–3

1. 250	2. 537	3. 607	4. 607	5. 973
A10	T28	L4	L487	C78
Religion	Science	Technology	Technology	History

Activity 5–4

1. 400–499
   C
2. 500–599
   F
3. 200–299
   F
4. 900–999
   G
5. 800–899
   B

Activity 5–5

1. C. a book telling how a polio victim overcame handicaps
2. C. a play
3. B. an inquiry into the architecture of American housing developments
4. B. the story of medical help for the blind
5. A. a book dealing with word origins

Activity 5-6

1. author, title, subject
2. *The World of the Great Horned Owl*
3. Ronald Austing and John B. Holt, Jr.
4. Lippincott
5. 1968
6. pure sciences
7. Ronald Austing and John B. Holt, Jr.
8. 158 pages
9. Living World Books
10. Answers will vary.

Activity 5-8

Titles of reference books and page numbers will vary. Following are some possible reference books and answers to the specific questions.

1. almanac; 45.3 meters or 151 feet, 1 inch
2. biographies of actors; November 10, 1925
3. atlas; Mt. McKinley, 20,300 feet; Death Valley, 282 feet; difference of 20,018 feet
4. encyclopedia; Arabic
5. dictionary; Latin
6. *Granger's Index to Poetry*; James Russell Lowell, "The Vision of Sir Launfal"
7. Answers will vary.
8. Answers will vary.
9. Answers will vary.
10. almanac; 1920; Warren G. Harding

Activity 5-9

Answers will vary but should look something like this:
"The politics of owls." Bill Lawren. il. Omni. V9 pg. 40.

Activity 5-10

A. *Motor Trend*
B. *Women's Sports & Fitness*
C. *USA Today*
D. *Sky and Telescope*
E. *Science News*
F. *Rolling Stone*

Activity 5-12

UNIT REVIEW

1. A. Lo
2. B. author card
3. B. Walter Lord
4. C. The good years
5. D. all of the above
6. B. 973.9
   Lo
7. A. nonfiction
8. Harper
9. 1960
10. pictures
11. C. subject card
12. A. the Da drawer
13. B. Don Cash Seaton
14. B. *Physical Education Handbook*
15. B. 790
   SE
16. Prentice-Hall
17. 1965
18. fourth edition or printing
19. C. Charts may guide return from moon
20. C. both of the above
21. H. Taylor
22. *Time*
23. 89
24. 51
25. June 25, 1986
26. New way of living
27. A new kind of country
28. *McCalls*
29. 105
30. May 19, 1987

OTHER NTC SKILL BUILDERS

What You Need to Know about Reading Comprehension & Speed, Skimming & Scanning, Reading for Pleasure: 0-8442-5176-3